AUTHORIZE *it!*

Think Like A Writer

To Win At Work & Life

DEBORAH BURNS

Advance Praise for

Authorize It!: Think Like a Writer to Win at Work & Life

"*Authorize It!* decodes storytelling structure to make it accessible for non-writers so everyone can craft and tell their stories."
—Samantha Skey, CEO, SHE Media

"A revelatory path that offers everyone the opportunity to lead their careers rather than the other way around."
—Philippe Guelton, President of Crackle Plus &
Chicken Soup for the Soul Entertainment VOD Networks

"Whether you're reimagining the job you have or imagining the career you want, this book transports you directly to the work that fits your life!"
—Kathryn Sollmann, Author, *Ambition Redefined*

"*Authorize It!* unleashes what is deeply rooted in all of us so we can create and share our own stories, and best tell the stories we need to at work."
—Robyn Moreno, Storyteller, coach, and founder, *Get Rooted*

"Now more than ever, success requires fresh thinking. This unique approach offers a new perspective that will help to get you wherever you want to go."
—Francis Cholle, Founder, The Human Company and
WSJ best-selling author, *SQUIRCLE*

"A brilliant, meaningful, and accessible framework for transformative growth that anyone can activate. The author's approach is at once inspirational and practical, an invaluable combination."
—Joanne, Heyman, Founder & CEO, Heyman Partners

"A remarkable, substantive, illuminating approach that uncomplicates personal narratives and business storytelling."
—James Hall, Dean, University Studies Division, RIT

"Understanding and activating the power of storytelling is crucial for leaders across all industries, and this is the book we've all been waiting for."
—Sharon Napier, Chair + Founder, Partners + Napier

"Full of gems!"
—Anna Figueroa, Board Member, *Girl Be Heard*

"*Authorize It!* workshops shift mindset and enhance results—now this companion book offers everyone the chance to better navigate their career stories."
—Amy Wilkins, CRO, *Smithsonian Media*

"An original and essential talent development approach for enlightened leaders and their teams. It's a powerful responsibility for us to keep paying it forward and have a purpose to our passions."
—Kathi Sharpe-Ross, CEO & President, THE SHARPE ALLIANCE, and author, *RE:INVENT Your Life! What are You Waiting For?*

"In an era where strategic storytelling is misunderstood, *Authorize It!* is an accessible playbook for all."
—Natalie Nixon, Author, *The Creativity Leap: Unleash Curiosity, Improvisation, and Intuition at Work*

"Practical guidance that takes the abstract and makes it actionable—better communication is a game-changer in your career and your life."
—Jane Hanson, Emmy Award-winning Journalist, Communications Guru, and Host of *See Jane*

"The author is such a strong innovator and a bold writer. Her advice is sure to set you up for Big success!"

—Ann Shoket, Founder, New Power Media, and author, *The Big Life*

"These profound lessons reveal how a writer's mindset will help you to plot your career moves and evolve into the best version of yourself."

—Fran Hauser, Startup investor and author, *The Myth of the Nice Girl*

"If you want to live up to your full potential, plot your best career, and positively impact every scene in your work story, read this book right now."

—Romy Newman, President & Co-founder, Fairygodboss

Dedicated to the minds who inspire me,
the hearts that touch me,
and the hands that guide me.

"Nothing is more powerful than an idea whose time has come."

—Victor Hugo

TABLE OF CONTENTS

Backstory: A Novel Approach

Everyone loves a good story.

What is it about stories that affect us? Of course, they are entertaining. But on a deeper level, a story, like art, connects us to our essence, to fundamental truths about ourselves and the world we inhabit. And that makes them powerful.

Stories offer us perspective about life by showing what's underneath the surface of our everyday realities so we can make sense of our experiences. Epic tales grab us precisely because they *reflect* what is universal in all of us and we, in turn, can relate.

To touch our hearts while keeping us on the edge of our seats, stories are deliberately plotted to mirror the same components, human needs, and emotions that we encounter over and over—dreams and disappointments, desires and fears, rivalries and resolutions.

What follows is simply this: If stories are structured just like life, then *life must be structured like a story.*

Introducing *Authorize It!*—the process by which we all can harness the power of storytelling to craft our own next chapter, thrilling sequel, surprise ending, and hard-won triumph. It is an entirely new way of looking at the world, built on the secrets that all good writers know but most people outside of that rarified realm do not.

By using the same creative principles that guide writers when they construct a captivating story, you can enlighten yourself and enhance your professional success. And the good news—especially since the task of writing for publication is reserved for the eccentric or tortured few—is that I'm not asking you to *be* a writer. You simply need to *think* like one.

Thinking Like a Writer

How-to books and tools for writers abound, from drafting bestselling novels and screenplays, to developing characters, stronger beginnings, tighter middles, and bang-up endings. But since ninety-eight percent of people are not writers and never intend to be, they don't benefit from all this available knowledge, or even consider that this wisdom might be applicable off the page. Yet the story techniques used by writers can help us in the real world. And there is no better backdrop for a great story than the real world of work. Part palace life, part rumor mill, and part ant farm, our careers consume one-third of our waking lives. Whether you live to work or work to live, what we do—and how we do it—gives us so much more than security. Work is tightly woven into our identities and wellbeing; it gifts us competency, meaning, and hopefully fulfillment. So, we all need this dose of wise counsel to ensure that we live our best work lives.

Viewing yours from a *story structure* perspective will empower you to take the reins of your career and manifest what you want with greater ease. *Authorize It!* breaks down the writing process and makes *thinking like a writer* your mindset and filter for everything so that you can move your story forward in any way you choose.

Applying the *thought-process* of a writer to your life helps you to understand yourself and others more deeply, spark new ideas and approaches, and hone the stories you need to tell for success. The wisdom in these pages will:

- Shift the way you view your life at work so you can live up to your true potential.
- Clarify your responses to the obstacles you will inevitably face.
- Focus you on your goals while keeping you open to what's new and dynamic.
- Improve your creative problem-solving and questioning.
- Cultivate your power to lead more boldly, innovate more productively, and connect more authentically.

Why Now?

Storytelling can transform your approach for a new era. The 21st-century workplace is shifting dramatically as technology accelerates, margins thin, businesses consolidate, and jobs as we know them—and the skills they require—continue to morph. We are moving from a world of thousands of large corporations to millions of untethered individuals doing their own thing. In all this uncertainty, one certainty is crystal-ball clear: whether you work for a company or for yourself, you will need to become more entrepreneurial if you are to flourish.

And you will naturally become more self-directed and inventive once you develop your storytelling muscles. This single commitment is crucial to your success, especially in our post-pandemic, volatile world. Now more than ever, cultivating the power of story will not only help you to stay afloat but to ride the waves, hold onto your vision, and ultimately come to a shore that you want to land on.

You will be able to protect and preserve your career by infusing the ability to develop your own story—your personal brand—and to create, pitch, and promote ideas in a way that will get you noticed. Whether you are in-office or remote, a corporate or contract employee, a solopreneur or freelancer, a manager or manager of a side-gig—or someone who's just trying to balance work within a well-rounded life—*Authorize It!* will get you to where you want to go.

My Story

I know just how transformative the lessons in this book can be because I experienced them first-hand when I became a writer and learned that, more than just helping me to craft a story, they flowed into every aspect of my life and career.

Growing up, I loved nothing more than reading and writing (in truth, they were the only two school subjects suited to my imaginative nature). I excelled in them, but since I struggled in almost all of my other classes, the scales tipped to average.

When I got to college, I majored in journalism and set my sights on being a reporter. Newspapers—remember them?—seemed like the best way to channel my talents. I wanted to be just like comic strip heroine Brenda Starr, the red-headed ace reporter in a man's world who managed to break every story.

I worked on my esteemed college newspaper, LIU's *Seawanhaka*, writing and editing news articles, and in my senior year even rose to become its first female editor in chief. But when I graduated, newspaper jobs in New York City were scarce and it seemed unlikely that I would realize that exact dream.

Instead, as the 1980s began, I entered the glamorous world of women's magazines. Not on the editorial side as I had envisioned, but on the business side—the operational engine of it all. After months of job hunting, I accepted a role at a small advertising agency that had several major magazines as clients. In my two years there, I was surprised by how much creativity there was on the marketing side. Having learned that, I didn't hesitate to join the circulation marketing department of *New York Magazine*. The opportunity to work on such a prestigious brand—and to be a part of its story—was incredibly exciting.

Eventually—even though I never saw it coming—I was able to switch publishing companies twice more and move into corporate marketing. I spent my days dreaming up ways to engage with the female readers of our magazines and brainstorming ideas for the outside companies and brands who wanted to connect with them. It turned out to be better than I could have ever imagined. I continued on to eventually oversee *ELLE* International from the U.S., and ultimately to lead brands like *ELLEgirl*, *Metropolitan Home*, and *ELLE Décor*. For someone who loved words and writing and using powerful content to have an impact, I was living a dream career.

Just when I really hit my stride, however, the publishing world began to implode. This was over ten years ago at the crest of the digital revolution when print magazines looked their digital future in the eye and did not know what to say or do next. The business model changed and suddenly everything needed to be reinvented—*fast*.

A new role was created to help guide us through the tumult, and I became the company's first chief innovation officer. I was in totally new territory with an urgent mission to help shift the corporation and create whatever was next. Even though I gave that inventive role one thousand percent, publishing everywhere continued to hemorrhage.

Finally, my company was for sale, and my career—a foundational pillar of life as I had known it for twenty-five years—just melted away. I was adrift, with no job, no lifelines, no easy solutions, and no vision for what to do next.

Revelations

Just when it seemed as if I had hit rock bottom, three surprising events helped me to rise from the ashes.

First, after a lot of reflective soul-searching while trying to get myself unstuck and back on track, I decided to become the chief innovation officer of *me*. Instead of being wedded to a corporation replete with its own issues, I would be the master of my own fate. I began to carve out a new professional space as an independent media consultant specializing in brands that needed to be reinvented—and I was one of them.

Going from being an insider to a lone outsider was a terrifying leap. On the flip side, when you've lost all your anchors and everything around you needs to be reimagined, anything is possible. I hoped that I was on a new path leading me somewhere and sure enough, another publishing company soon hired me to help them reinvent one of their sagging magazines. To do so, new products and services would be required, so I once again dove into women's hearts and minds to discover what they needed, and then collaborated to bring new initiatives to life.

Still, as much as I knew about what 21st-century women wanted, there was one woman in my life whose heart had always remained a mystery to me—and that was my mother, who had passed away twenty-five years before. All my "hit-rock-bottom" introspection as I looked back on my professional journey to decide where to go next also led me to revelations about my complex relationship with the woman I loved best.

As I thought more about who she was and how she had shaped me, I found myself wanting to write about her and our story. It felt like the only way to both preserve her memory and to better understand our relationship —the creative in me itched for a new project; the daughter in me felt that this was something I had to do.

When I first stared at that blank page, I had no idea of where I was going, or even what I was doing. I'd always had a way with words, first as a journalist and then as a marketer, but writing a book—well, that was entirely new territory. Being raw and honest about who she and I were together sometimes felt like emotional torture and recognizing the amateurishness of my first draft was a torment of its own. But that initial spark led me on a twisting, turning creative journey of learning and self-discovery until seven years later my memoir, *Saturday's Child*, was finally published. The whole experience—the shaky start, the gratifying finish, and all the bumps along the way—made me see both writing and myself in a new light.

As it turned out, the process of putting my life into narrative form gave me a completely new perspective on life *in general*. It not only forced me to reevaluate my personal history and the people in it, but also the significance of almost everything I had done or encountered up to that point. Suddenly, I saw reasons, connections, and motivations between people and events that I had never really considered before. I understood how I had adapted to challenges and harnessed my own talents and resilience in the face of obstacles to succeed.

And then, once the book was published, another lightning-bolt moment hit. As I traveled around the country talking to women about my story, I found myself articulating what I had learned from my immersion in the world of writing. I realized that despite having been a chief innovation officer, despite having led teams and projects, and despite consulting with many different companies, there were five lessons about leadership and success that I had never known—or at least fully realized—until I wrote a book.

It had taken my creative journey to crystallize what had been hidden from me all along. For the first time, I saw how the marriage between my left-brain business expertise and my right-brain creativity gave me the capacity to adapt and reconfigure everything that had come before. The *Authorize It!* lessons were the secret sauce behind my smooth transition from corporate life to consulting life to author life. In fact, I realized that I had lived my entire life by these lessons. Somehow, they had been hard-wired, guiding me over the years—without my even knowing—and I suddenly knew that they could benefit others as well.

With newly minted credentials as a Certified Professional Coach (C.P.C.), I began sharing my "think like a writer" method. A feature in *Thrive Global* quickly expanded to workshop programming for hundreds at libraries, and then to thousands of employees inside of corporations. *Authorize It!* was making its way into the world, and just as I had benefited from this unique path to success, so did others. The exponential power of activating all five lessons was playing out in real-time before me—mindsets were changing, new visions were forming, and positive testimonials were building.

So inspired, I created an online course that, over time, will reach thousands more. And everything that I have learned from career coaching and from my entire journey is now packaged into this second book that you're holding.

It all started when I decided to "author-ize" my life—and now you can too.

It's Time to "Right" Your Story

When it comes to your own dreams and ambitions—and to the path that you desire to unfold before you—I am here to tell you that you hold the pen as the writer, protagonist, star, director, and producer. You do not have to *write* your story as I did but thinking about your life as if you were going to turn it into a book or a screenplay will bestow on you the power to *right* it.

All stories have a central theme or high-stakes question at their heart, surrounded by a structural framework that holds all the characters and plot points—just like a digital or product wireframe at work. Your story also has a central theme at its core that is contained by its framework. So how do you understand and influence the structure that is shaping your story? How do you discover and impact its theme so that your story becomes the one you want to live? By following the five *Authorize It!* lessons:

7

1. **Embrace the Narrative Arc**
2. **Understand Your Characters**
3. **Welcome Conflict**
4. **Seek the Unconventional**
5. **Step Into the Unknown**

These lessons are explored in the chapters that follow and will help you ascend to where you want to be. Each lesson comes complete with actionable takeaways that you can use on Day One and forevermore, as well as additional tools including:

- *Prompts*—Writers use Prompt exercises to get their ideas flowing, and each one is designed to propel you into action.
- *Authorize It!* **Live**—True Q&A stories compiled from women I've coached that demonstrate how to apply the wisdom in the chapters for even more successful outcomes.

As you begin to embrace the lessons and think like a writer, you will recognize your own power to enhance the story you are living—over time. Unlike condensed episodes or stories that tie-up neatly and resolve after two hours or four hundred pages, life unfolds gradually. Change does not happen overnight, but as you shift your approach and surrender to your story structure, change will come, sometimes in tiny increments and sometimes in big, beautiful, crashing waves.

My greatest wish is that once you have the *aha* moment and understand that life really is like a story, you will clearly see how to grab the reins for the ride and achieve the level of success you want. So I invite you to consider me your personal consultant and coach as I clarify for non-writers how storytelling can enhance your professional and personal life every day.

Lesson One: Embrace the Narrative Arc

Even if you are not a writer, you've no doubt experienced the power of storytelling. And the essential spine of every single tale—the structure that moves the plot along and keeps us turning the pages —is called, in writer's terms, the Narrative Arc. If you are more used to Venn diagrams, bar charts, bell curves, and spreadsheets at the office, don't worry. Just think of a Narrative Arc as a timeline that illustrates how stories rise, fall, and progress.

There is only one difference with a Narrative Arc chart—the story arc cycles being tracked are always, always the same. Whether it's *Hamlet* or *Harry Potter*, *Titanic* or *The Marvelous Mrs. Maisel*, *Jaws* or *Big Little Lies*, all stories follow the oh-so-familiar pattern of ups, downs, pushes, and pulls. Yes, the settings and events change, and the characters are as infinitely variable as the different beginnings, middles, and ends, but the formula of any great story remains constant (otherwise it wouldn't be great).

If you peel away the distinctive outer trappings, you can count on finding the familiar stages of status quo, catastrophe, and transformation underneath. It all boils down to this: a person (or a company) is living life and then something rocks their world, then rocks it harder, then pushes them to a point of a crisis, then rock bottom. And eventually, there is an emergence and ultimately an evolution.

For those who think in terms of visuals, Narrative Arcs can be mapped in a straight line, circle, or inverted U-shape to convey the turbulence that is part of any tale. All of this was first codified by professor and scholar Joseph Campbell in his book, *The Hero Has A Thousand Faces*, and then re-explained in his seminal work *The Hero's Journey*. Campbell was fascinated by folklore and mythology, and he formed his theory by studying the components of the myths and stories that had sustained humankind for centuries, which is why the pattern he identified is also known as "mythic structure." From Native American and Greek mythology to the stories of the Bible or the Bhagavad Gita, he mapped all their similarities and predictable occurrences. Many others have since elevated Campbell's work, including Hollywood screenwriter Christopher Vogler in his more recent classic, *The Writer's Journey*. In fact, after Vogler wrote a memo about Campbell's structure when he was once working as a story consultant at Disney, it swiftly became the conscious framework for nearly every Disney movie.

Structure: The Four Stages

Since I'm assuming that you're not actually planning to *write* an epic but to *live* an epic life, you will need to take Campbell's theory and make it practical and actionable so that it can be applied to your circumstances. In my own experience, a story's structure can be distilled into four key stages that form the Narrative Arc's almost seasonal cycles:

> *SHIFT:* Something changes the landscape, which creates a problem and establishes a goal.
> *INSTABILITY:* New uncertainties and realities emerge from the unfamiliar terrain.
> *DARKNESS:* Despair hits as more about the goal is known and tests/ challenges mount.
> *LIGHT:* Resolution follows an intense struggle, and then there's an evolution.

The plot—with its individual events and turning points—is what moves us along the arc's trajectory in a way that keeps readers or viewers engaged. At work, there are concurrent storylines—your boss's for example—that impact yours, and these follow the same stages. In fact, unlike a finite movie or book that focuses on a single challenge and its resolution, your work world is more like a television series with numerous, connected stories, each with its own Narrative Arc that begins and resolves season after season, project after project.

If you don't understand the Narrative Arc structure, it can be hard to view the cycles that you are experiencing as a natural part of the process that will lead you to the next phase of your own evolution. Instead, when you hit the stages of Instability and Darkness, you can feel stuck, hopeless, and riddled with fear. When you understand the four stages, however, you are more likely to believe that there is always the opportunity for a new plot twist and, when you are faced with difficulties or headwinds, to remember that they are a natural part of any journey and that a solution will always appear.

Discovering My Arc

After there was a Shift in my work landscape and I started writing my memoir, I thought I knew my goal: to understand and preserve the memory of my other-worldly beautiful, elusive, larger-than-life mother—whose pedestal I, as an only child, had danced around all my life. It seemed straightforward and yet, true to any hero or heroine's journey, it turned into a life-changing adventure that lasted years.

When I first began writing, I did double time, waking up at ungodly hours to write before heading off to my day job. Mastering the craft of writing was also a challenge. I learned that what worked in my old world of magazines did not work in this new world of writing book-length narrative non-fiction. My journalism degree and business marketing background had wired me for the headline or the tag line that would engage people. So, my first inclination was to sum the story up in a prologue that basically gave away the ending. I knew that was wrong, but I was uncertain about how to move forward because I didn't know how to write any other way. This was my stage of Instability. I knew that if I wanted to find my footing, I needed to immerse myself in longer stories and other memoirs to look closely at *how* they were told.

Finally, I decided to give up everything else—my consulting practice, revenue, time, *everything*—to complete the book. The last two years of my journey were spent in total sacrifice to my quest. I moved from spending my days in the New York City world of corporate boardrooms to the aloneness of my suburban Long Island dining room table. I traded heels for loungewear and contact lenses for glasses, with my eyes staring at a computer screen seven days a week.

From my immersion in the literary world—and through practice and persistence—I honed a writing style that slowly unfolded my mother's story piece by piece and scene by scene so that readers could climb on board and understand her character and her life's events. But when I was about three-quarters of the way through, I felt something was off. I began showing it to early readers who confirmed what I feared most: that this love letter to my mother wasn't working.

That's when the Darkness cycle hit, and it all seemed hopeless. The book began as a way for me to immortalize her, but at that nearly finished point my early readers picked up on what was missing. Their insights made me realize that as the writer, the real story was about me and my own emergence from her shadow. The story wasn't working because the only way an outsider could understand, or come to care about, my mother was *through me*—I needed to be at the center as both the narrator and the central character. Then readers could jump into the action alongside me to experience our relationship and what it was like to be her daughter, and to understand who I was at the beginning as a child versus who I ultimately became.

This stunning realization was critical from a writing perspective—and for my own evolution. All this time, I had seen my mother as the heroine, but as it turned out, the heroine's journey was actually mine. For the story to work, I not only had to envision myself as the heroine, but I also had to look closely at how my actions, reactions, and expectations had been formed by the woman who shaped me.

What it really meant in terms of my writing was that, after all this time and effort, I had to start over and reframe the story as my own. There are no shortcuts to writing and self-discovery and sometimes, a do-over is just what's required. I went through all the cycles of the Narrative Arc on my creative journey—which meant that I endured tremendous highs, terrible lows, and more turning points throughout than I can count. But when the book was finally finished, I came into the Light.

That entire process taught me much about life, about work, and about how we perceive ourselves and the hands we are dealt by fate. It has underscored for me the power of agency and our ability to write our futures and push forward even when the road is dark.

My new creative life has shown me that storytelling is relevant to all of us and can be harnessed to propel us forward in whatever we choose to do.

YOU are the Protagonist

Why do you need to know all this? Because you are the heroine or hero of your personal story—and as the central protagonist, you too need to chase the career and life you want on your own Narrative Arc. This path will almost certainly take you through periods of Instability and Darkness—the two most challenging but absolutely necessary phases. Remember how people initially wanted to just "cancel" 2020 because of that year's uncertainty and unrest? But then some started to see that the crises of 2020 might grant us a unique ability to envision a better future—a catastrophic year that we needed to emerge from so we could grow. Without the pain, there truly never is gain. Always keep in mind that stories imitate life—and in stories, Darkness always leads to transformation and triumph in some way.

So how do you become a heroine or hero who can successfully navigate the challenges built into your own work world? By developing an *H Mentality* (for ease from this point on, I'm referring to the heroine or hero within you as the H). And the most impressive H's possess five essential characteristics that ultimately help them to evolve as they seize each day:

-   **They have spirit.** Enthusiastic and solution-oriented, H's act in memorable ways, even when they are fearful or facing adversity.
-   **They have perspective.** H's have open minds (even about themselves), objectively consider all sides, and focus on the greater good.

13

- **They are inquisitive.** H's are innately curious and are willing to be lifelong learners.
- **They are empathetic.** H's are sensitive to those around them, accepting imperfections in themselves and others.
- **They are sincere.** H's are true to their word, authentic, and dedicated.

As the H, if you work to strengthen these qualities in yourself at every turn, you will stand-out and win.

Building Your Arc

There are four key ingredients in every master Narrative Arc: **Quest**, **Action**, **Reaction**, and **Expectations**. Think of them as your flour, sugar, water, and eggs—by combining them, you will have the foundation for almost anything you'd like to cook up.

Ingredient #1—THE QUEST

When some inciting incident, new situation, or problem shifts your "ordinary world," that moment establishes your quest. Every H has something they're seeking, and your stated goal or desire is what defines the road ahead. Similarly, what your company is chasing is established by some shift in the environment that will lead to new objectives. At work, both the individual and the company revolve around what is desired: the end goal, the winning pass.

Think of your quest as *your intention*—when everything you do is in sync with a defined intention, you are more likely to have a greater impact, help your company overcome its obstacles, and get what you want. A quest is akin to the central story problem every author tries to resolve, and at work, there will be a problem your own quest seeks to overcome. To get the best story result, writers first define the story problem and then set a quest for their characters that focuses on the solution. In other words, writers are quest-centric—forward-looking, positive, and proactive—rather than negative, reactive, and problem-centric. In the *Wizard of Oz*, for example,

14

Dorothy's problem is that suddenly she's not in Kansas anymore. If author Frank Baum framed his H's quest in a problem-centric way, she would probably languish in a foreign land with no way out. Instead, Dorothy's quest to return to her loved ones is proactive and forward-looking—she sets off to meet the wizard who she believes has the power to get her back home.

Framing your own quest like a writer will yield better results. Let's say you're trying to overcome a lack of adequate compensation. A problem-centric intention would be, "I need more money." A quest-centric intention would be, "To learn these three new skills and justify my next raise." Once you have defined your problem, focus your quest as a writer would—on *what you will do* to overcome it.

Then, just as Dorothy did as she traversed the yellow brick road, stay open to all the new that pops up on your journey because quests can morph along the way. As your intention, it is a flexible high-level vision of what you want for yourself, not a rock-solid detailed plan. Still, it is crucial to identify your problem and your quest upfront because they fuel and filter everything.

Aligning Quests

Whether producing works of fiction or non-fiction, writers must focus at the outset on what exactly their H is after. Since your universe is your work world, exploring how your personal quest intertwines with your company's quest is critical to your ultimate success.

In *Succession*, the HBO award-winning series about a family-owned media empire, son Kendall has a powerful quest: to emerge from the shadow of his ruthless father by building different business opportunities for a new world to finally earn said parent's admiration. However, the company quest set by his father is to become the number one global media entity by doubling down on tried-and-true, traditional tactics. Kendall believes that success will take new thinking which, unfortunately for him, is in direct opposition to his cutthroat father's belief. The result?

15

> Kendall's personal quest and the company's quest do not align, so chaos and power plays ensue!

At work, you may be facing a constellation of quests—simultaneous macro and mini-quests that combine to propel both the larger Narrative Arc as well as smaller story arcs forward. There are always multiple projects and competing priorities that all seem to need chasing at once. This can make it hard to know what to focus on, so you will need to get grounded at the beginning—here's how to *authorize* finding and aligning your quest:

Priority One: Establish your personal quest at work
- What is it that you want (or at least what you think you want/need right now)? Your goal could be to earn that raise or a promotion, to expand your skillset, to switch departments or industries, to maybe one day be the CEO, or conversely, to have flexible hours to build a side-gig or to spend more time with your family. Think about what success looks like for you (for a long stretch when my children were young, more family time was what it looked like for me, so I carved out—pioneered, actually—a three-day in-office schedule). Ask: *Do I need to reshape any plotlines or patterns at work to get me where I want to go?*

Priority Two: Understand your company's quest
- What is it that your company wants (or the company you might want to work for one day)? Every business has a growth mindset and a macro-quest that will deliver that growth year after year. Their quest guides their executive action and kicks-off objectives for individual departments. If you're not sure what it is that your company is chasing, take a look at their mission/values for their overarching goal, and then think about the goals your manager has set for you. Ask: *What is my role in their story, what value do I add, and what leverage might I have?*

16

<u>Priority Three: Examine how the two intersect</u>
- Do the quests align? Seeing where they are in sync and where they might differ in a way that blocks your progress is an important forward step. Just as with any partnership, if both parties' desires are not in sync, it will be harder to attain the success you want. And since a total alignment is more fantasy than reality, it will be important to ask: *Can I fulfill their objectives while staying true to my own?*

Ingredient #2: ACTION

As with everything in life, companies are in a constant state of change. Competition abounds, technology accelerates, business models disrupt. No one needs to shout "Action" in the hallways because it's always a mad scramble.

A writer knows, however, that a story has to constantly be *moving forward*, or else it's probably not a story worth telling. As you assess your work life, look at it through the frame of action. If you're not taking steps to move something forward for yourself *and* for the company every single day, then you're showing up but not really *acting*—and your story will grind to a halt. Writers innately understand the importance of movement when plotting their stories and the best ways to tell them. Great writing has a rhythm to it; it is like music or even choreography—the dance begins not when the dancers take the stage, but when they start to move.

At the office, it's not just *movement* that's required, but also continual *improvement*. Writers write, then rewrite, revising and perfecting as they go. So just like writers polishing their stories, everything you touch at work—every project, product, meeting, or opportunity—needs to be finessed by you and made better just because you were involved.

There are three levels of action that require your conscious attention daily. Think of them as simultaneous storylines in the same way a novelist has multiple plotlines. Devote yourself to each and you will shine as you propel your company's quest forward:

17

- **Quotidian.** Diligently execute your day-to-day job responsibilities that keep the business humming, working smarter as your arc unfolds and you continuously improve. This should take up fifty percent of your time.
- **Inventive.** For those daily responsibilities, formulate new approaches, strategies, and tactics that will lift the bottom line. Think about Amazon offering same-day delivery—what needed to change for them to make this promise real? Steady improvements to what you are responsible for should take up thirty percent of your time.
- **Visionary.** Creatively brainstorm entirely new plotlines (i.e.: business opportunities, possibilities, collaborations, and ventures) that blend your specific area of expertise with all of the new things you are learning or hearing about in the world around you. This should take up twenty percent of your time.

Have a notebook with you wherever you go and write down your to-dos, meeting notes, questions you want answers for, conundrums you want to solve, and anything that sparks your imagination. Put a **Q, I,** or **V** in the margin by each note to identify which activity category it falls into. Refer to your notes each day to take some action, and you'll be on your way. And remember, the virtual keyboard is always beneath your fingertips—you can delete, revise, and course-correct at any time based on new information or a change in priorities.

The Four M's

No matter what your position or quest, these four M-words—culled from the way writers move their stories forward—will help you build momentum and get you noticed:

18

Matter. Writers know that every character must contribute to the story—otherwise, they have no reason to be there. Since you are the H, you must add value to the equation at work. Make a difference.

Manifest. Be present and visibly demonstrating something every day. Both stories and life require consistent effort, perseverance, and persistence in order to become real. Be an ideator and an implementer.

Measure. Writers break stories down into manageable parts—scenes, chapters, acts one, two, and three—and you need to do the same to move your ideas or projects forward more effectively. Take small steps for big progress.

Mold. The confines of the Narrative Arc framework are actually freeing for writers because its structure makes it easier to pace and plot stories. Ironically, wild out-of-the-box ideas happen more frequently when writers operate within the "box" of the arc's structure. So for your big ideas at the office, have a defined framework with boundaries, milestones, deliverables, and timelines.

When there is continual action and then progress, you achieve momentum. Momentum is key for both stories and business. You can feel it happening in your bones when a project wakes you up in the middle of the night because your head is full of ideas; when an initiative catches fire and suddenly resources and buzz start coming your way; when one client spawns another and then another. That's when your story starts unfurling like a book that's impossible to put down.

As you strive to move the plot of your story forward, make sure that your quest informs and filters what you do. Let your intention guide your actions every step of the way for the greatest impact.

Ingredient #3: REACTION

Just as with any tale, the protagonist's *response to the action* throughout is what moves the story forward either positively or negatively. As the H, your response to the plot points of your life is one of the most critical aspects in shaping your personal and career stories.

In other words, *how you choose to respond*—especially when bad things happen—is the ultimate determinant of your success and wellbeing. When you face the inevitable obstacles and setbacks that will come your way, your reactions will be harder to control. Why? Because there's usually emotion involved.

What you do next when you're faced with a rumor that your department is being eliminated, or your boss slashes your budget, or someone else gets your dream job can either be productive or counter-productive and can have long-term consequences. And it's not just about your external reaction that others can see, it's also about how you internalize, perceive, and process what just happened.

Modulating your reactions at work—that is, adjusting, tempering, and fine-tuning how you engage—makes the process of reacting *active* rather than passive. By doing so, you turn a reaction into an action that can build momentum and move your story forward. Just as a writer puts the right words into the H's mouth, what you do and say has meaning—your words and behavior can keep the momentum going or thwart it. To be your most effective self and accomplish your end goal, be aware of what is happening around you, stay flexible, and adjust as necessary when you engage with others. When you are intentional in your responses, you'll have a better chance of winning.

The Four R's

Whenever you are called upon or are compelled to react, keep these four R-words in mind:

Respect. An office is an ecosystem, and you are one character in a world populated by many others also there to earn a living. Appreciate the feelings, needs, and dreams of those around you. Be mindful of the hierarchy in place, how it works, and how you fit in. Honor it, even if you might want to change it one day.

Reconsider. Writers make use of quiet and solitude to turn inward for inspiration and to produce their best creative work. Give yourself time to reflect before reacting; press pause before sending that email and edit your verbal and written communication before it goes out into the world. In short, think twice.

Restrain. Listen more than you speak, and, as always, consider your actions. We live in a sensitive and expressive age where opinions are readily and widely shared. But impetuous comments and imprudent demands are rarely to anyone's advantage at work. Remember why you're there and play the long game to win—you will have many chapters in your Narrative Arc to solve your problems and achieve your goals.

Realize. The gradual nature of how a story unfolds—of incremental gains only after losses, of two-steps forward and one-step back—make patience a necessary edict, even though it's diametrically opposed to our generally impatient selves. One of the many reasons that we love stories is that they allow us to learn more quickly through someone else's challenge. But since we live in real-time, we must realize that answers, resolutions, and experience can take years, if not decades, for us to acquire. To react appropriately and overcome the inevitable disappointments in our own Narrative Arc, we must see this clearly.

Ingredient #4: EXPECTATIONS

As every H lives and perseveres through the challenges of their own story, the ability to manage expectations is critical. Yet as a culture, we seem to be losing the resiliency to get over the normal humps and bumps. In an accelerated, voyeuristic, social-media-driven world, we expect things to be great, perfect, fast, and easy. And when they're not, we often find ourselves crushed and disillusioned.

So know this: emotional tumult is a given, as are regular problems and predicaments *even when you are on the right path*. You cannot go the distance between point A and point B in your Narrative Arc or succeed in your quest without going through the stages. The sooner we accept that challenges are always part of the mix and manage our expectations accordingly, the better prepared we'll be to handle whatever comes our way at work and in life.

Knowing the predictable cycles is both empowering and frightening. On one hand, you know that you are going to get through the lows, but on the other, you know that eventually the other shoe is going to drop, and it won't be pretty. However, there is a peace that comes with accepting—and *expecting*—that nothing will be achieved without challenge. This is true for every H, no matter who you are or what your backstory. Obstacles are forthcoming—as they are in any evolving story—but viewed positively, this also means that a new plot twist could be just around the corner.

The Four C's

You can keep your expectations real by following these four C-words:

Choose. Dissatisfaction rears its head when our expectations aren't met. And when they aren't met at work, internal pressure mounts because we wish that the present could be something that it's not. Choose to accept the moment you are in, and keep what you *actually expect* to happen reasonable, even low. Dream for sure, but also choose to see your reality and work with what you have as you keep moving ahead.

Concentrate. Hopes and expectations send our minds careening ahead, but at work, handling the current moment is critical. No H ever knows how the story is going to end, so focus on the journey or the task at hand rather than on outcomes to avoid disappointment. Celebrate the small wins along the way and focus on them, rather than where you're supposed to be at the end.

Collaborate. You cannot control others, only yourself. So while you should always convene with colleagues and empower them to do their part, don't have unreasonably high expectations for them. However, through your own actions and reactions, you should always work to exceed the expectations that others have for you.

Clear. You may feel strongly that something *should* happen or as if you're the one who is right. But since there are so many variables that go into office decision-making (just like storytelling), you should open yourself up to the possibility that you may not be. Stay clear of trying to prove something, of controlling others, and of trying to manage someone else's agenda.

Now that we've seen how your life—how everything—is a story composed of quests, actions, reactions, and expectations, let's zoom in on how it all plays out at the office.

At Your Desk

A corporation, a department, a project task force, or a committee within any company is nothing more than a group of people on a collective quest. Any team is an ensemble cast with a plotline of its own, and what happens on the journey to complete a project from beginning to end follows the same predictable story trajectory. There is always something that we—or our bosses—want or a problem that we need to solve, and there are always intended and unintended consequences from our actions that need to be dealt with.

As you strive to gain clarity on your two quests—your personal journey and your company's—know that all writers continually ask themselves *What is the story I'm telling?* with each chapter to ensure that they don't lose their way. For example, as *Jurassic Park*'s characters face the chaos of dinosaurs unintentionally let loose on the world, the movie's central story question is: Can humankind control nature? It's the high-level, universal question we all can relate to; it's the throughline from the beginning until it resolves at the end, and it hangs in the air during every scene.

High-level story questions apply to business too. For any company to succeed, they must be able to ask—and answer—the right questions:

- What business are we in?
- What is the core problem our business solves?
- What is our unique value proposition that allows us to solve the problem?
- What is our mission and who benefits from it?
- How do we best share the vision of our story to our target audiences: employees, customers, clients, and partners?

Once upon a time, the great American camera manufacturer, Kodak, was one of the most powerful global companies. But soon after the millennium, technology's seismic shift was beginning to be felt in almost every industry. At this critical juncture, Kodak didn't ask themselves the central story questions, and they didn't react with a new quest. In fact, they didn't do anything but deny that they were in the midst of radical change.

If only they had viewed themselves as the makers of *memories* rather than specifically cameras and film, they could have potentially invented the camera phone or at least supplied the camera components for it and remained formidable. But they held firm to their legacy manufacturing story —and lost almost everything.

Conversely, computer manufacturer Apple wove a conceptual story. Instead of focusing on their particular products, they zoomed out to articulate their vision. Apple's highest-level story began with the expansive line: "Think Different." Those two words established their creativity, aligned them with genius inventors who changed the world, set the bar for their employees, and set the stage for a stellar line-up of products beyond computers (which, of course, included the memory-capturing iPhone).

Every company's outer journey includes a set of problems to solve, which in turn gives the characters within the story the opportunity to offer creative solutions. Circumstances can turn dire when consumer behavior suddenly changes or when marketplace competition threatens a firm's very survival. Or it can be as basic as switching to an open-office environment that causes an employee uproar at the outset. As with all stories, things will get worse, then worse again as obstacles abound. Then, suddenly—through actions and reactions—a glimmer of hope or, at least, learning for a better future. And finally, there will be growth and evolution that translates into a hopefully successful outcome.

The Four E's

Here are four E-words to ensure that you positively impact your company's Narrative Arc and make progress on your own:

Excel. Set your intention to consistently do your absolute best. Always stretch higher and constantly do more than situations require. Over-prepare, give it your all, and never, ever wait to be told what to do. Maximize the positive, minimize the negative, and be a solution machine.

Execute. We know stories break down if the protagonist doesn't act, and at the office, implementation remains the key to success. Just as your actions must yield something, continue to remember that a great idea is just a great idea until you make it real. How? By executing on your quest every single day.

Embody. There are times in every story where characters act like more than what they actually feel. Always act "as if" you are the H you aspire to be. Look, walk, and talk the part. Know your value, build relationships with everyone, emulate the best traits of those around you who you admire, and be an example that will help them grow too.

Evolve. Stories evolve, and so must you. Make yourself smarter at every turn. Volunteer for committees, give a hand in another area, help when you don't have to just so you can learn something new and deepen relationships.

Your Next Step

I promised at the outset that you wouldn't need to *be* a writer, just *think* like one—so don't panic when you see the exercises below.

Reflection is integral to understanding your story, so you do have to get some things from your head to the page or the screen—in fact, writing them down in some fashion is an essential step in making them real. But no one is ever going to see these notes because you're not writing for publication, you're writing for you. So let's *authorize* it—grab a notebook or start a documents folder that you can use solely for our exploration together. Then begin answering the Prompts below that are designed to help you fully comprehend and *Embrace the Narrative Arc.*

Prompts

Ponder. In the same way writers continually probe about the story that they are telling, consider your own story's themes. As your first *What's My Story?* step, make a large diagram divided into four parts for each of the stages of the Narrative Arc—Shift, Instability, Darkness, Light. Then recall one situation from your past where you lived through the four cycles and write down what happened in each one of them (Note: if you have more than one momentous life event that you want to track, create a separate diagram for each, but you need to complete at least one).

Shift

Instability

Incident

Darkness

Light

Probe. As you begin to establish your work quest, you may be uncertain. So, in addition to asking yourself what it is that you want in your career, make a list of all your related and unrelated talents, skills, and interests. Are you a musician, mathematician, and magician? List them all and consider *the threads that tie them together*—what do they say about who you are?

Identify. Think about the major plot points in your life that have led you to where you are now, and what a twist in the road might look like. Visualize standing at that crossroads, then list three small steps (or plot points) that can get you closer to a new direction.

Identify. To make room for the Inventive and Visionary levels of daily activity, list your top ten Quotidian responsibilities from your job description. As you review each one, think through possible ways that you can work smarter to free up your time for the bigger picture thinking that will get you noticed.

Map. Think about a recently completed project that you worked on. Make that same large diagram with the four stages of the Narrative Arc—Shift, Instability, Darkness, Light. Summarize what actually happened in each cycle and see how the project unfolded according to the pattern of the Narrative Arc. Now add three lines springing out from each of the four stages. On the first, state what your expectation was, on the second, state what actually happened, and on the third, your reaction. Ask: *Were my expectations in sync with reality? Could I have reacted differently to the action and gotten a better outcome?*

Shift   *Instability*

Darkness   *Light*

Map. Come up with one idea that you know could help your company (or use one new idea that's already underway) and map it to the stages on a new Project diagram, along with what *could* happen in each one. Draw lines attached to each quarter detailing the major steps that might unfold in the Narrative Arc cycles. Imagine yourself as the instigator and think about how you can take positive action and resolve any problems that could crop up. From presenting the idea to your boss to its successful conclusion, you want to see yourself at the center of the action.

Shift

Instability

New Idea

Darkness

Light

Imagine. We focused on your personal story with the first *What's My Story?* Ponder Prompt, now this Imagine Prompt is your *What's My Company's Story?* exercise. To deepen your understanding and help your business storytelling, answer these Narrative Arc story questions: *What cycle are we in now? What is our quest, our client's quest, and our customer's quest? Do they align and what are their commonalities? Do our actions, reactions, and expectations properly support our quest and the problem we are trying to solve for our customers?*

Authorize It! Live

Lesson One

"I so often feel aimless where my career is concerned. I'm twenty-eight and secretly ashamed. Almost everyone around me seems to be side-gigging and multi-hyphenating their way into fantastic futures. They've found their passions, and all their talk about their successes makes me feel as if I'm not driven at all. Truthfully, I don't know how ambitious I really am, but I do know that nothing seems to happen for me. Seriously, I can't even answer what my passion is, let alone my quest. Am I hopeless?"
Sharon

Sharon, you are not alone! How to find your true calling is probably the most common career discussion topic of all time. It's not only your generation—raised with high expectations and a belief that anything is possible—that struggles with facing ordinary realities. So many suffer from an "is-this-all-there-is" feeling of stuck-ness, and I hear this same complaint over and over when I talk to women of all ages.

Since your question reflects such a popular ennui and uncertainty, we'll continue to explore it throughout with additional lesson insights at the end of each *Authorize It! Live*. For now, let's put the writerly wisdom in Lesson One to work for your own Narrative Arc.

Shift. I believe that for you, the first cycle has actually happened already. Your inciting incident is the shame that you feel, and your quest has already been launched—to find what you are most passionate about so you can build a career and live a life that you are proud of.

Instability. You are now in this second cycle and experiencing the emotions that will ultimately jumpstart you into action. You know something needs to change, life feels shaky, everyone seems to be surpassing you, and you're unsure of which way to turn. All of which are completely normal feelings at this stage. Let's begin to build your Narrative Arc using the four ingredients.

- **Quest.** Put aside the idea of a "passion" for the moment and try to get clearer about what it is that you believe you want: Independence? Financial success? Acclaim? Flexibility? Meaning? Also, what is it that you value most: Family? Friends? Adventure? Security? Spontaneity? Solitude?
  - Then ask yourself what suits you about your present role and what doesn't.
  - While you're at it, identify some inspiring career role models and businesses.
- **Actions.** First, fully accept that you don't need to know what your calling is to begin to change. Shift your mindset from waiting for the passion to appear, to beginning to bloom where you are planted now.
  - Adopt the five H characteristics, and take small, daily steps to make each of the traits real for you.
  - Apply the four E-words in this lesson that affect the Narrative Arc and stay attuned to their positive impact. You may not be totally happy where you are working, but no matter. They have the power to change the dynamic of your story and how you feel about it as well.
  - After doing the Identify exercise in the Prompts, take action on the three Q-I-V storylines approach—you will begin to feel a subtle change even amid uncertainty.
  - Now, it's time to move forward by taking small steps using the four M-words.
    - In meetings, determine one thing that you can do to add value—and then do it.

32

- Make one change to how you structure your day and then add this one: spend ten minutes on LinkedIn every morning. Just explore, keep up with what's changing in your network, and connect with at least one person you might want to talk to someday. While you're at it, search for anything that interests you online, and click each of the top ten search results to see where they lead you.
- Be hyper-aware of what you do. Keep a daily log of three actions you took and what happened. If you were unhappy with any of the outcomes, note what you wish you had done or said instead that might have changed the result.

- **Reactions.** With the four R-words in mind, let's take some concrete steps to shake things up and generate action through reaction:
  - Remember "Opposite Day" at school? For one day each week, do the opposite of what you would normally do: say yes when you might have said no; say no when you would have said yes; express a thought when you might have remained silent.
  - Convey enthusiasm by simply smiling all the time (if you do this already, don't stop!)
  - Ask someone at your company how they feel about a work issue, or for their perspective on something you're working on.
  - Let go of a problem that tests your patience and give it room to breathe.

- **Expectations.** Your question expresses your expectation that you should be a driven, ambitious person. As a result, not feeling that you are makes you operate from a place of lack rather than feeling "enough" just as you are now.

- Walk yourself through the four C-words in this lesson to help ground you in the present moment.
- Believe that you are right where you're supposed to be. Keeping your expectations in check while being grateful for everything will help shift you into a beneficial abundance mindset.

Darkness. Because the answers you seek will not come overnight, brace for a period where things will appear even bleaker. There might be a trigger —a friend becomes the youngest VP at her company, or another starts her own business that takes off, or you get passed over for a lateral internal move —but through it all, you must remember it's a part of the process. These plot triggers have a purpose. They're there to stress you and to test you and to make you more resilient—take heart in the fact that calm waters do not sharpen a captain's skills, only rough waters do. You will need your H traits —your Spirit, Perspective, Inquisitiveness, Empathy, and Sincerity—now more than ever as you muddle through the Darkness stage and build a foundation for your evolution. No matter what happens, continue taking small steps toward something. As long as you keep adding plot points to your arc, you will be moving forward on your quest and things will start to happen and change.

Light. Keep at it and you will reach this stage where at least a version of the passion you are chasing is caught. Through the genuine excitement for whatever it turns out to be—and from all the learning gleaned from navigating your Narrative Arc—you will find yourself transformed in some way.

Lesson Two: Understand Your Characters

S tories elicit an emotional response—we love them precisely because they are written to make us feel something and share in experiences that we never would have otherwise. And what we feel comes to us through the characters who are propelling the story. This is why writers focus so intensely on the personas they create, with all of their many facets, good and bad. The primary character, of course, is the protagonist, so he or she will typically get most of the writer's time. But even though you are the H and protagonist of your story, you are not a one-person show.

The greatest forces affecting your quest may be *other people*, and they can certainly have a dramatic impact on your work life. Sometimes their role is obvious, sometimes not, but if you are going to succeed it is essential that you try to understand the characters around you. Only then will you be able to harness the helpful ones while skillfully managing the ones who complicate your goals.

Your Supporting Cast

Human nature and needs are the drivers of everything at work and in life, and therefore anyone who crosses your path will have their own perspectives, agendas, and motives. If you don't make the effort to grasp the individual and group dynamics around you, you cannot move forward or lead as well as you might.

Our expert in narrative structure, Joseph Campbell, has identified the most common character archetypes that are found in stories alongside the protagonist:

- The **Mentor** who appears and offers guidance, advice, and support to the H.
- The **Ally** who assists the H on their journey, like a sidekick.
- The **Shapeshifter** whose motives are unclear and who can't quite be pinned down as either for or against the H.
- The **Trickster** who adds humor and is in the mix to shake things up either positively, negatively—or potentially both.
- The ever-present **Antagonist** (a.k.a. villain or shadow character) who clearly is out to get you.

Each one contributes something different to your story and has a depth and complexity that you need to acknowledge. For example, it's easy to view those mean antagonists negatively since they seem to exist just to block your path. But the presence of an antagonist will always teach you something about yourself that you wouldn't know otherwise. Ironically, you need antagonists and other stressors in your story to evolve and become your best, most-developed self.

The Character Arc

Just like each story has a Narrative Arc, there is a parallel Character Arc as well. Characters go through cycles of emotional upheaval, struggle, and change in sync with (and in addition to) what is happening to them in the larger world. The same push-pull quality that we find in the Narrative Arc also exists within the Character Arc, and the predictable stages of Darkness and Light appear as the protagonist and the other characters in the story struggle mentally and emotionally to deal with obstacles.

Since writers need to know their characters inside and out, they often create detailed backstories for them. Many of these elaborate histories are never revealed, but they help to shape the character's personality and motivations, as well as how they act and react in different scenes. Great writers purposely keep secrets; they hold back so that the reader or viewer can insert themselves into the story and interpret situations and people on their own—and this is true in life as well. But as the central character, it is

36

up to you to assess these people around you with the skill of an investigator in a mystery and discover their quests, actions, reactions, and expectations in order to facilitate your own.

Playing Detective

In the real world, characters don't come with subtitles on a screen to make deciphering their words easier. And in books, the same holds true. Instead of *telling* us that a particular character is dishonest, or jealous, or destined to be a savior, writers use descriptive language and scenes to *show* us that a character possesses these traits. Telling you that a character is angry is boring. Writing vividly about veins throbbing and faces contorting, on the other hand, is exciting and puts you right into the story. *Showing vs. telling* is one of the literary world's most fundamental principles. Great writers express what is bubbling beneath the surface to show how the character feels, which enables you to feel and interpret those same emotions.

In your work world and in life, you need to read the people around you as if they were appearing in the pages of a book and use the same interpretive process that you would as a reader to figure out what is happening and why. Your capacity to discern—to recognize fact from fiction; to determine what is worthy of attention and what is not—is a power that you need to activate and hone over time.

Sleuthing

As you observe, keep in mind that most things fall into one of three categories and it can sometimes be hard for even the most astute sleuth to tell the difference between them:

Perceptions. Everyone around you will *show* you who they are over time. They won't tell you (and if they continually tell you who they are, be suspicious). Pay attention to clues as you tune in closely to your co-worker's traits and temperaments, actions and reactions, and what they show you about their character.

Imperceptions. We humans are a trusting bunch and it's often challenging for us to truly determine what and who we're dealing with. Continue trusting, but as the saying goes, verify. There's always more to the story—part of the iceberg is always hidden below the surface and the true meaning of events is often not readily apparent. Make sure you look hard, read between the lines, and look behind the scenes to best decipher the real story.

Misperceptions. Because the whole truth is rarely evident, signals easily can be misunderstood. A story that you initially perceive as fact may actually be incorrect, just as a story that you imagine to be true may live only in your mind and might not be true at all. Be willing to give someone the benefit of the doubt, and just like a writer, strive to be a non-judgmental, uber-observer.

So study the characters in your story and think about what role they play based on the different persona archetypes. Is your boss a mentor or an antagonist? What makes them successful in this position and what might undermine them? Watch for signs, acknowledge your gut feelings, and listen more to what is *unsaid* than said. Attempt to be an impartial spectator or a wry bystander—just like a writer would. And like every author, tap into what is universal about this person's story: is there any aspect of their experience that you can relate to? Is there anything about them that generates empathy or sympathy? This type of understanding and sensitivity will allow you to connect with them more deeply.

Why is this connection so important? Because relationships are vital to succeeding and ascending at work. In fact, apart from your own mindset and moves, relationships may be the most important factor in whether or not you achieve your quest. Everyone is on their own journey with their own quest, and everyone wants to have input and to be involved. They are the H's of their own lives and at the center of their own action—to them, you are the supporting character.

So if you want to succeed, you need to leave space for them in your story to bring them along with you. This applies to co-workers and bosses, vendors and freelancers, customers and clients, or whoever else you interact with and rely on to reach your goals. Switch to a "we" when communicating with them so that they feel united with you and your ideas, and with what you and your company want to achieve. Give credit to others freely and be sure to call them out by name when you mention their input. By leaving room for them to contribute to your story, they will feel good—and that will help you to ultimately win.

One hint: your own vulnerability and relatability are the keys to building strong relationships, just as they are for characters that we bond with in stories. Authors know that these two qualities are essential for any protagonist if they are going to win people over. And these traits can help you to diffuse any competitiveness or resistance your supporting characters may feel towards you based on their own insecurities. So as the H, be sure to project both.

Know Thyself

Your Character Arc speaks to your inner journey, one that transpires simultaneously with the action that moves the plot along on your Narrative Arc. This is your emotional evolution, and it necessitates a psychological deep dive to discover inner needs that may be entirely unknown to you.

As a reader or viewer, you have probably noticed that the protagonist often begins the story confused or clueless about what he or she actually needs to make changes and evolve. You may be in the same place. Remember the son Kendall from *Succession*? At the start of the series he had none of a hero's traits—he was so far from being heroic, in fact, that he began the show as what's referred to as an "anti-hero" (which, truth be told, is how many of us feel). But rest assured that every character journey permits the H to start out one way and then emerge wiser and more mature on the other side.

In their workshop titled *The Hero's 2 Journeys*, storytellers (and story fixers) Christopher Vogler and Michael Hauge describe this ever-present inner arc as moving from "being defined by others to defining oneself." They believe that an H's transformation is "the process of shedding a mask, or false identity, and becoming our true selves, or essence." As you begin your own discovery process, this powerful idea about the parallel Character Arc bears repeating: Your personal journey is about changing from *being defined by others to defining yourself.*

We are all in a constant state of flux, of molting and becoming. And we are all products of our own flawed histories, which simply means that just like any character, *we're all flawed.* Even your most stunningly confident co-workers or friends who appear to be living a perfect life make mistakes, have bouts of unworthiness, and fear failure. Therefore, we carefully construct social masks that present us as closer to perfect than we actually feel.

Akin to vulnerability and relatability, accepting our shortcomings is a must because they are a part of what makes any character, even an H, appealing. Writers know that characters are best received when they are sympathetic, and the imperfections that we try so hard to hide are often, ironically, what make us this way. This paradox is best illustrated by the Japanese art of Kintsugi, where broken objects are sealed back together with gold, so the cracks are visible and become a part of the piece's story. The paradigm-shifting lesson for us is that our broken and imperfect places can ultimately turn out to be our strength and a large part of what connects us to others.

As you move along your journey's path, know that it can be difficult for us to recognize our progress when we're in the thick of an unfolding story. On the contrary, we frequently feel as if we're going absolutely nowhere. But that feeling can be a cue to pause and probe. Asking yourself the following questions will shine a light on your forward motion:

- *How have I evolved so far in my Character Arc (perhaps without even noticing)?*
- *What aspect of myself can I now leave behind because I'm done with it?*
- *What new aspect can I keep and make part of my story going forward?*

The Long and Winding Road

Psychologist Carl Jung calls the process of becoming our whole selves *individuation*, and he believed that to complete the process, we all need to "reclaim and reconnect with the parts of ourselves we have orphaned over the years." This is precisely what happens on a character's inner journey. We all have a mythology of our own, built on the stories that shaped us. To reclaim ourselves and our power, we all must dive deep to uncover and face the truth about our history and the forces that made us who we are.

When I wrote my memoir, I stepped—almost by accident—onto the long and winding road to make sense of my past. As I looked backward at my relationship with my mother, I realized that I needed to question the stories that I had told myself about everything that had come before. New York Times bestselling author Dr. Brené Brown looked at her own family roots and said: "When I wiped the nostalgia off to uncover the real trauma behind many of those stories, I began to understand why we didn't talk about emotions growing up. This affects the ability to be vulnerable and needs to be reclaimed." This type of reflection and reexamination pertains not only to our family history, but to all the other relationships, hardships, illnesses, or difficulties that we have faced. Every single one of us has interpreted and misinterpreted events from our young lives. We told ourselves stories—that may or may not have been true—to protect our own helplessness, to distract us from our fears, and to make sense of the incomprehensible.

Not only can these stories hold us back, but they can also run deeper than just the parents and children in one household. Epigenetics—the study of how our genes can change their expression without changing their structure—has opened the door to considering the possibility that we can *inherit* generational wounds. Author Mark Wolynn's *It Didn't Start with You: How Inherited Family Trauma Shapes Who We Are and How to End the Cycle* posits that we can all be affected by and carry the wounds of our ancestors. In other words, we can unconsciously strap the unfinished business of those who came before us on our backs, leading to everything from anxiety and depression to irrational fears and addictions.

When I was writing, contemplating the history that my mother and I shared from a distance of twenty years made it easier for me to reconsider what had happened between us in a positive light. Growing up, I never felt like a priority or fully loved, but digging deep into our relationship—and the relationships and events that had shaped *her* into the woman she became—allowed me to break free from that limiting belief. I realized that what I had held onto all of my life as true may not have been true at all.

The writing process also helped me to fully grasp just how I had emerged strong from a dynamic that could have rendered me weak. I saw how her narcissism and my longing for her attention had ultimately given me skills that served me well in life. Constantly trying to figure her out had helped me develop my intuition and a unique awareness of people's needs and emotions. Trying to win her affection had made me creative and resourceful; adapting to her mercurial nature had made me flexible; putting her at the center of my world taught me to help others shine. And holding on tightly to hope for all those years—the hope of being worthy of her time and love —had made me extremely resilient. I could get knocked down and get back up again, like a fighter. My wounds had actually turned into secret weapons that I packed in my toolbox every day for use at work and in life. Suddenly, I was living a brand-new story. She was not the mother whose love was always just beyond my grasp. She was the mother I needed to become who I am. *Thanks, Mom.*

The key to unlocking your own inner journey is to first recognize and then seek to resolve any events and burdens from your childhood that may still affect you today. When you can make sense of your past and understand who you are now as the H, every aspect of life—especially the world of work —will become easier to master.

Rewrite

These three steps will help you with this process:

Step #1: REFLECT

Your suffering and challenges make you the H you are, so take a closer look at what drives you, and why. Contemplating not only yourself but also the other characters in your life to better understand their actions and reactions are important steps. Reflecting on the whole of you and them—and on what they may have also faced at the time—can be healing while it builds empathy, which can shift your perspective.

Step #2: REEXAMINE
Try to look back at the hardest situations and most painful experiences objectively, not in a lamenting way. Attempt to revisit these scenes from your life without rage, shame, or blame, all while holding up the possibility of forgiveness.

Step #3: REFRAME
As author and coach Tony Robbins says, "Life doesn't happen to you, it happens *for* you." So see the inherent value of your mistakes and wounds. Find your own way to be grateful for the lessons they taught you and how the places that once felt broken in you might actually have developed into strengths and assets. Examine and internalize the positive contributions these perceived flaws have had on the person you are becoming.

As you understand yourself more deeply, you will start to more clearly see the H you have been all along. Once you know your character's starting point, you can begin to ascertain how you need to evolve in life to bolster your contentment and success.

And one final note as you take stock of your emotional history. It's not just the hard struggles that are worth examining, so pay attention to all the good as well as the bad. There is much to be gained from looking at the moments when you felt happy, connected, and fulfilled. You need to understand what moves you toward joy as well as what might hold you back from it. As you reflect, reexamine, and reframe, try to strike a balance between the two so you can more easily distinguish what you don't want from what you do.

Crafting Your Starring Role

The process of becoming whole, of your character's evolution, is a lifelong one. Ideally, our lives are just one big character journey that culminates with us as our wisest, authentic, and most highly evolved selves. To achieve your best self—and to become your absolute best incarnation as an H—*Authorize It!* by following these four writerly guidelines:

Guideline #1: EDIT YOURSELF

We know the vital role that editing plays in the literary world, as well as in the worlds of film and television. Applying an editorial eye to your ever-changing story and character is a useful mindset, especially with your career. Understand that each day, you are building the story that you're telling, and self-editing how you act and react is crucial. Think carefully and frequently about the character you are now and the character you might want to become. You can start by asking:

- *Do I approach my work and relationships with integrity?*
- *Am I doing anything that contributes to drama or holds me back?*
- *Am I a reliable narrator—do I tell myself and others the truth?*

Company Edit

Even if you are not responsible for creating your company's story, you can edit it for clarity and simplicity to help you focus. Almost any company's mission and message can use an EDIT:

E = Explain the character you serve (the customer).
D = Describe their problem.
I = Illuminate the solution you provide.
T = Tell how your solution will make your character better.

If you complete this core edit for your company and begin to use it as a filter for what you say and do, your conversations will improve because you tightened your focus. Editing anything down to its essence will help

Guideline #2: FIND YOUR VOICE

All writers strive to have a unique voice—an identifiable, individual style on the page so they can express themselves in a singular, original way. At the office, think of this as your personal style of communication. Once you've identified the character you want to be, it's time to figure out how that character interacts with others and articulates ideas, so know that:

-   All writers edit for the audience they serve. At work, think of your reader—your audience—as the CEO of your company, or your investor, partner, or client. Even if you're giving the most minor presentation to a peer in an informal setting, the quality of what you are communicating should be the same as if you were presenting something to that high-level executive.

-   As they are in any novel, your words are your prime communication mechanism, and they are powerful. When writers are first starting out, they must learn how not to express a point three ways: to say something, say it again a different way, and then again. What you really want to do is get to the single most compelling thought, so draft it in your own style and voice and then continue editing it for precision. As William Shakespeare said, "Brevity is the soul of wit."

-   The goal is for you to know your message so well that you can be flexible enough to improvise and tailor its essence to make it resonate with any audience. And strive to understand different styles of communication. Change up your language and style so that you meet people where they are—in other words, frame your message so it can be received in the best possible way. For example, if you are talking to a financial person, lead with a story woven by data; if you're talking to a creative, inspire them with a vision. Even the most complicated point will resonate as long as you distill it to its essence and are savvy with your delivery.

- As the H, your job is to always package things with a neat beginning, middle, and end so that the story moves forward. Here are some tips for using your voice to propel action and plot points:
    - **Make** it easy for anyone to understand the situation, and then to act.
    - **Make** any communication more fascinating and engaging by infusing stories.
    - **Make** it a practice to never present a problem without a germ of a solution.
    - **Make** your boss's life easier at every turn—in fact, make everyone's life easier.

Guideline #3: CONSIDER POV

Often, writers struggle with POV—or point-of-view. Through whose perspective should the story be told? As the H, your point of view is paramount. However, you will get further if you attempt to understand the POV of the other characters in your story. You may have a storyline in your head that you believe is factual, but someone else's perspective may present an entirely different POV that can help you see an event or circumstance— or yourself—in a completely new way. The insights you glean by getting inside their heads can help you act and react more effectively down the road. So never hesitate to ask the simplest of questions: *What's your perspective on this?* And then listen.

POV Pointers

The next time you go to a meeting, play a game in your mind. Pretend that you are each person around the table and summarize what happened in the meeting *from their viewpoint.*

How did they feel about the co-workers around the table or on the call?

46

Did the meeting go as they had planned and are they happy with the outcome? Did they want to shine, and did they succeed or fail?

Remember that the other characters in your work story can be picking up *your* POV vibes too. Great tales begin with a protagonist who consciously or unconsciously yearns for something new—perhaps she is in a situation that she has outgrown and, as a result, feels a certain restlessness, dissatisfaction, or longing—all of which can be silently (or not-so-silently) conveyed to everyone surrounding them. This can be good or bad, so be aware and always ask yourself: *Am I conveying what I want others to see?*

If your POV is negative or angry, keep it to yourself until the time may be right to express frustration. Remember, you can say almost anything to anyone, it's how you say it that counts. However, not everything *should* be said—in fact, some things should remain unsaid if you do not expect them to be productive for you. In other words, don't express something at the office just for the sole purpose of getting it off your chest. Instead, collect your thoughts to determine if this is a frustration that, once expressed, will get you closer to something that you want.

Your filter question is: *How would this serve my quest, move my story forward, and help me to win?*

Finally, the POV of your company will determine its success. As our EDIT shows, a business is not the H of their story—the customer they serve is. No matter what product or service they produce, a company is a supporting character—an ally or a mentor—who exists to help guide their H customer to the solution for their problem. If they see it another way—if their POV has them at the center of the story instead of their customer—

they will not be as successful as they could be. Help your company to see this and to tell their story from that POV and you will push your own work story forward.

Guideline #4: DIFFERENTIATE

Writers must differentiate their characters so that readers and viewers can tell them apart, anticipate how they will behave, and love them or hate them. Recognizing your commonalities with others at work will help you to solidify relationships, but to stand out as the H, you must also distinguish yourself from the pack. What do you bring to the table that is unique?

Think about the myriad products on just one shelf in your favorite supermarket. If all the cereals were alike, you could choose any box—blindfolded, no less—and it wouldn't matter. But they're not alike. From Cheerios to Wheaties, Shredded Wheat to Raisin Bran to twenty new-and-improved alternatives, they are all *marketed by their differences* from each other. Discovering what distinguishes *you* and then leveraging those qualities will help you to stand out at work and get your contributions noticed.

Focusing on your hard skills is a clear way to distinguish yourself (you have this degree, you've worked for that company, etc.), but focusing on your *soft skills*—that is, interpersonal traits and talents like initiative, leadership, teamwork, and cooperativeness—is what will garner the most attention in a work ecosystem. With that in mind, here are some ways to bump up those soft skills to become a true H who is set apart:

- **Give.** Always, always help someone else freely, without being asked and without expecting anything in return. Even when you are seeking something from someone, never take without also giving back to add value to every conversation. Genuine giving of yourself lifts the soul and comes back around in meaningful ways.
- **Listen.** Hear, see, and try to understand the people around you so they feel validated.
- **Go.** Tackle something that everyone else is avoiding.

- **Trust.** Be that person everybody trusts; refrain from gossip and be true to your word. Absence of trust is a major office disruptor, so be an authentic H, even if you're the only one.

At Your Desk

As we've seen, zooming in on who you are, the forces that have shaped you, and who you aspire to be is critical to your transformation and success. Now, it's time to really grapple with these three inner journey career questions:

- *Who do I understand myself to be?*
- *Who do people understand me to be?*
- *What, if anything, do I want to change about the story I'm telling?*

To do this, we're going to play a game. We know that every author has to profile their characters so they can get inside their hearts and minds. Now it's time to *fictionalize yourself.* Who are you as a character? Think of yourself and the circumstances of your life in the third person as if you were standing outside of yourself, watching your life on-screen at a movie theatre. This objectivity from on-high will help you to identify your inner storyline and further solidify what you want your Narrative Arc to be.

Why do it this way? Because it's so hard for most of us to answer direct questions about ourselves. It's liberating to shift to an imaginary realm and pretend that you're talking about a fictional character. But in the same way that a fiction writer's work is based on nuggets of truth from their own life, your answers to this third-person approach will still reveal different aspects of you.

So start by asking yourself the Protagonist Profile questions below as if you were developing a character for a novel or screenplay. Describe what makes this star character who they are, how they laugh, who they love and hate, what motivates and scares them. Try to be as honest and unfiltered as you can be, and don't overthink. Your first thoughts are what we're after.

Some of what is revealed may be eye-opening; other answers and emotions may not be entirely new—you may already know them deep down in your heart. But this profile will hopefully help you to more clearly see your positives and negatives, as well as any blocking or limiting thoughts. By seeing what has fashioned you and what jazzes or deflates you, you'll more deeply understand what has brought you to this place so you will be better able to move forward. You don't want to keep repeating plotlines that have not served you, or ones that you have now outgrown because you're ready to move on from that version of yourself.

It's time to binge-watch the original series that is your life—with you in the starring role. See it, feel it, and know that you have shaped your story this far by your choices, actions, and reactions. Most importantly, you now have the power to *rewrite it* should you so desire.

Protagonist Profile

1) What is your H's character, personality, and temperament?

_____

_____

_____

_____

2) What are your H's five positive traits and five negative ones?

_____

_____

_____

_____

3)   What are three things your H enjoys and does well?

_____

_____

_____

_____

4)   What are three things your H hates and avoids?

_____

_____

_____

_____

5)   What does your H value most in life?

_____

_____

_____

_____

6)   What's the best thing that ever happened to your H, and the most terrible? (If there's more than one, what do they have in common?)

_____

_____

_____

_____

7)   What are your H's daily habits and routines? Describe a day-in-the-life.

_____

_____

_____

_____

_____

8) What does your H want to change, and what habits keep that change from happening?

_____

_____

_____

_____

9) What is your H's biggest dream, biggest inner conflict, longing, or need?

_____

_____

_____

_____

10) How does your H's life philosophy, ethics, morality, duty, or religion affect this character?

_____

_____

_____

_____

11) Who most shaped your H's childhood, both positively and negatively? What did your H learn from each?

_____

_____

_____

_____

12) What is your H's secret fear or wound? What negative belief does your H secretly believe is true?

_____

_____

_____

_____

_____

13) What is the identity your H presents to the world? Does your H have emotional armor?

_____

_____

_____

_____

14) What would your H say to their younger self and future self?

_____

_____

_____

_____

15) What does your H want more than anything?

_____

_____

_____

_____

16) How will a reader see this character? Will they like or dislike your H?

_____

_____

_____

_____

17) What does your H do for a living? What would it be if finances, education, or responsibilities were not a factor?

_____

_____

_____

_____

18) When other characters turn to your H, what do they seek most often?

_____

_____

_____

_____

Now onto the other important characters in your life. This next portion will help you to better understand what role they play and how they affect your story to set the stage for viewing them—and your issues—in a new light.

Supporting Characters

As you continue to stand outside of yourself, identify the people at work or in your life who are your supporting characters—Mentor, Antagonist, Ally, Shapeshifter, and Trickster—and answer these five questions for each one who you can think of:

1) What is their role (or what could their role be) in the unfolding story that is your life?

_____

_____

_____

_____

2) What do you think motivates this person and are they aware of their inner needs?

_____

_____

_____

_____

3)   Do they have too much or too little influence on you? Why?

_____

_____

_____

_____

4)   What is it that *they* want from you?

_____

_____

_____

_____

5)   What can you do for them?

_____

_____

_____

_____

As you ponder your answers to the Protagonist and Supporting Character Profiles to help develop your story, let's revisit those three inner journey questions. Answer them now with any new insights about yourself in hand:

Who do I understand myself to be?

_____

_____

_____

_____

Who do people understand me to be?

_____

_____

_____

_____

What, if anything, do I want to change about the story I'm telling?

_____

_____

_____

_____

As we end this second lesson, pause to review all your answers and note any revelations, patterns, or themes that surprised you. Is there one big takeaway for you? Is there one small step that you can take to make it real? Is it possible to reframe a belief that is holding you back?

Now, onto this lesson's exercises that will further strengthen you and your Character Arc.

Prompts

Ponder. Revisit Lesson One's *What's My Story?* Narrative Arc depiction of how you lived through the four cycles of a particular incident. Now extend a line from each of the four parts and write down the *emotion you felt* during each cycle. Then ask yourself: *Did my feelings change from start to finish? Was I stronger at the end than I was at the beginning?* Then extend two more lines from each cycle and write how that emotion made you act and react. Ask: *Did my actions and reactions reveal anything that could impact my character* *growth? Did I under or over-react? Did my emotions teach me something that could positively impact me going forward?*

Probe. Think about what makes you engage most with a character in a book, movie, or series. Pick one of your favorite H's and then ask: *Which of their characteristics can I infuse into my own life?* Then plot how that character morphs from who they were at the beginning to who they are at the end. Is there anything about their path that you can emulate—or avoid?

Probe. Wonder about your picks for a dream team at work. Why them? What are their complementary character traits? What traits do you bring to that dream team and what role could you play?

Identify. With differentiation in mind, how can you best shape the distinct character that is you? Is there something about you that makes you stand out—either positively or negatively? As you examine your answers, can a negative be reframed into a positive? List the attributes that make you different. Ever feel as if you didn't belong? Could the reasons why now be turned into assets?

Identify. Pinpoint a dramatic childhood moment that set you down a particular path or still impacts your sense of self today. Now draft a scene about it in a few paragraphs. Why is this moment important, and what purpose does it serve (positively or negatively) for your story today? Does the feeling that you still carry from it help you to move forward, or does it hold you back?

Map. Revisit Lesson One's Narrative Arc depiction of a company project. Now extend another line from each of the four parts and write down all the emotions you felt during each cycle. Then compare the feelings you experienced on this project with the ones in your personal arc. Note the similarities and dissimilarities.

Imagine. Building on your *What's My Company's Story?* Prompt answers, now let's "humanize" your company—think about it as a character and describe it. Then ask yourself: *What is our customer profile and who are they as characters? Who are our top three clients as characters? What about my company's mission or product story inspired me to join?* And the most important question of all: *Does my company realize that the story isn't about them, it's about our customer?*

Authorize It! Live

Lesson Two

"I feel as if I can't trust anyone anymore. For all the talk about corporate culture and people supporting each other, it seems as if there's more office sniping and sarcasm and back-stabbing than ever. I've tried to figure out why, but all I can come up with is reality TV! Sometimes, it feels like my co-workers are talking to a camera, kicking up drama, complaining, blaming, whining, and totally out for themselves. I really haven't changed, or at least I don't think I have, but almost everyone around me has. Maybe I'm just too sensitive or belong in another era."
Kelly

Kelly, it does sound as if you are very attuned to those around you, and it also sounds as if, in addition to finding a work environment like this incredibly frustrating, you might have been burned a few times by putting your trust in someone who didn't deserve it.

This type of staff behavior usually reflects how management behaves or what they are willing to tolerate, so you could hold out for new leadership. Or you could switch companies, but if you're right about how people have changed, you could just be trading one set of difficult characters for another. Whatever happens next, you will need to continue working with these people for the time being, so let's tackle this problem from an *Understand Your Characters* perspective.

You're already a keen observer, so we need to use these skills to move past the toxicity you see and feel unfolding before you. Let's zoom in first on the only character that you can change—you. I sense that you feel overwhelmed by all the negativity, and rightly so. But you also need to examine what your co-workers' bad behavior can teach you and how you can use it to evolve.

Character Study. Can you define the main people around you by archetype—are they all antagonists? Is there a mentor in there, or a sidekick who sees things your way? What perceptions or potential misperceptions do you have about each of them? If you look more closely, is it possible to see something that you might have missed before? And while you're at it, give yourself a second glance. Since everything and everyone is in a constant state of change, try to pinpoint how you might have changed in your time at the company.

Crafting Your Starring Role. The power to control the situation rather than having it control you is in your hands. That is, in essence, what H's do. Recognize that you are in the midst of your Character Arc evolution and use the four writer's tricks—Editing, Voice, POV, and Differentiation—to adapt in a way that gets you through the day and enables you to rise above the drama.

- **Editing.** Other people have the power to make us edit ourselves in ways that we don't intend—if we let them. Are these untrustworthy sorts having an impact on the story you are conveying about yourself at work? For example, are you suddenly being perceived as an introvert, or boring, or not a team player because you steer clear of the toxicity? Or as judgmental because of how you respond? Ask yourself if you have been allowing others to edit you into someone you're not, and then turn the misperceptions around by consciously *showing* who you really are instead.

- **Voice.** Demonstrate your unique voice to co-workers by setting boundaries. Let people know, in a light-hearted but firm way, what you will tolerate. And by being fair. Without going overboard, make sure that you observe and listen to everyone. No one ever likes to be dismissed, and sometimes complaining will ease after people vent. And finally, by lobbing the ball—switch gears after a meltdown session and say: *I hear you but what should we do? Or: If* *you were in charge what would you do?* Try to get someone else to move past what's wrong and into what could be made right.

- **POV.** Right now, these negative supporting characters are drowning your own POV out, which only serves to silence and shortchange you. Instead of retreating, be sure to articulate the forward paths you see for any task or project next step. Then, be willing to listen to someone else's view and compromise, if necessary, to get yourself closer to the result that you want to achieve.

- **Differentiation.** Consider if all the chaos might actually be elevating you to management as the one solid person in the mix. Are you seen as the voice of reason? The person who keeps her cool no matter what? Having a demeanor suited for stormy seas can ultimately serve you well, so note all the positives that differentiate you within your office toxicity. Then own and demonstrate them at every opportunity.

A Follow-Up with Sharon from Chapter One:

Sharon, now that you've begun the process of uncovering your passion and your story's Narrative Arc, reflecting on your personal history and character will be helpful. Do the patterns in your life now feel eerily similar to patterns from other phases of your life? Have you felt this old familiar feeling before? Could you be letting others define you instead of defining yourself? If these questions are new for you, take comfort in the fact that you *will* get to where you're meant to go if you stay open and involved in the process.

First, use the Protagonist and Supporting Character Profiles in this chapter to help you envision your new starring role and ascertain where you as the H want to go. From one of your insights, commit to a single small step that you can take *tomorrow*. Also, try to positively reframe one negative belief you hold about yourself.

Then, work with the four writing world tips to finely tune the character that is you. Is there one new thing you can do to edit yourself, enhance your voice, express or change your POV, and differentiate yourself from the rest?

And while your story is unfolding on your own timetable, be sure to also pay attention to the other characters in your story—especially the ones that make you feel inadequate because of their drive or accomplishments. Ask yourself:

- *Why do they make me feel the way they do (and what's at the source of the feeling)?*
- *What do I think is driving them?*
- *Is there something I can learn from them?*

Lesson Three: Welcome Conflict

N ow that you understand how both Narrative and Character Arcs apply to you, let's move on to one of the most important elements that is entrenched in every single story: conflict.

A story without conflict, obstacles, antagonists, and high stakes is a giant bore. In fact, without something standing in the way of the H's quest, it's not even a story. At best, the resulting tale would be tepid, unproductive, and uninspiring. Without the stressors that goad us all to rise to a higher level, we might as well just sit back and bide our time going through the same motions day after day. Without death, there would be no life, as they say.

For a company, no conflict means no problem to solve, no problem to solve means no product, and no product to offer means no customers. Without external problems and the internal frustrations that fuel them, almost all businesses would crumble.

That said, many of us spend our waking hours avoiding conflict, not making waves, smoothing things over, and keeping everybody happy. But bumping up against an external challenge and finding your way around it not only keeps things interesting, it also builds resilience. Dealing with conflict is like invisible isometric strength training for your character that, over time, makes you into who you are. In fact, it is the lightning rod for your maturation.

This does not necessarily mean that you should seek out conflict, only that you should not run from it when it inevitably appears. Don't be afraid to shake hands with different personas, contrasting opinions, and whatever else you would normally avoid. Friction, handled with grace and civility, offers experiences that have the power to help us learn unexpected lessons and grow in ways we never thought possible.

The Shadowland

In fantasy or dystopian novels, the backdrops that spring from the writer's brain are often referred to as shadowlands. Why? Because these new realms are usually a metaphor for life's darkest conflicts and basic human instincts. From evil Gotham in the *Batman* series to Panem in *The Hunger Games* to The Republic of Gilead in *The Handmaid's Tale*, troubled universes full of struggle embody what we all fear. These jaundiced worlds meet the nefarious needs of Joseph Campbell's antagonist, who Carl Jung identifies as the "shadow archetype." And your life—whether you're in a difficult relationship or dealing with a toxic office situation—has the potential to be (or at least feel like) a noxious shadowland.

Even if you are fortunate to work for a company with strong leadership and an empathetic culture, your work environment will likely be populated with a few shadowy personas that stir up conflict and confusion. Their dark sides might be more obvious, but their shadow qualities exist in all of us to varying degrees—whether we are aware of them or not—and they rear their heads to make trouble in your office life.

External conflict, although rarely welcomed, almost always leads to positives, and this includes the sphere of interpersonal relationships. In their book, *Getting the Love You Want*, authors Harville Hendrix and Helen LaKelly Hunt are proponents of Imago theory—that your soul mate is actually not the companion who fits every possible ideal. Rather, your optimal match is the person who antagonizes you, challenging you to work through whatever wound you need to heal or obstacle you need to overcome in order to evolve. Think of all the rom-coms that screenwriters toil over: *When Harry Met Sally, As Good as it Gets, Hitch, It's Complicated, You've Got Mail, The Best Man, How to Lose a Guy in Ten Days*, the list goes on and on because opposites do attract and often powerful, unexpected things happen when they do.

All of this is to say that your antagonists, including the ones at work, are undoubtedly in your life for a purpose. Your job is to figure out what that purpose is and use that information to grow. From the boss you fear, to the back-stabbing co-worker, to the more successful colleague whose dust you are eating, all of them are there to help you work through and heal your issues so you can progress. Place this notion at the center of your work world and you will see them, your quest, and what's happening around you in a new light.

Embracing My Conflicts

I have a peculiar capacity to work with difficult people. In fact, I was dubbed the *Velvet Hammer* by my one-time boss because he felt that I could make things happen without angering even the prickliest personalities. I hadn't asked for this "gift"—and there were many times when I really didn't want it —but it was mine, no doubt a result of skillfully negotiating my mother's needs and moods for all those years. At times, I felt like a magnet drawing the obstreperous to me. Some of these unruly executives instilled fear and fueled confusion, all while kicking cans of conflict down the hallways. Yet often, their high-voltage temperaments—and the dysfunction created by constant drama—actually gave me opportunities to shine that I wouldn't have had otherwise.

I once worked for a CEO who didn't care who you were, what department you were in, or what level you were at—if he felt that you could make money for the company, he plucked you up and threw you right into the fire. Suddenly, an opportunity would appear that normally would not have been yours. Yes, one outcome was to fall flat on your face and get fired. But another was to succeed and rise through the ranks in a matter of months, whereas it might have taken you years to ascend to the same level in a more normal environment.

Once, long before the digital age, the notion of a customer database was just starting to catch fire. At the end of a particularly grueling meeting, I suggested to our CEO that perhaps we should explore the possibility of turning our simple list of magazine subscribers into a lifestyle database so we could better understand our customers and create new services they might want to purchase. In an instant, he put me in charge with the order to deliver a database in three weeks so we could present it to our number one client. I was in completely new territory fielding seemingly insurmountable obstacles at every turn. I don't remember sleeping much in those twenty-one days! Somehow, though, I got it done, nervously flew to the high-level meeting with our CEO, and presented the result. I knew that if it didn't go well, not only would the plane ride home be excruciating, but it would be my last day. Instead, it all went so well that I ended up with a promotion instead of a pink slip.

Living this way every day made me learn how to put out the fires. I also learned that being known as "a fixer" was incredibly empowering, as was being able to handle things smoothly where others might not have. Yes, I grappled with the realities of cutthroat corporate life and whether my nature was truly suited to its harsh underside. But at the same time, I realized that my interpersonal, negotiating, and tactical skills were being sharpened to a fine point. Being able to not only survive but to thrive gave me confidence, and all that conflict actually showed me what I was capable of.

Looking back, I see just how important that time was to my own evolution. Now, after living a creative life with more freedom and flexibility, I know that I could never go back and be content in that world. But the conflict I lived through and the challenges I overcame in those years taught me lessons that I still use today and made my new incarnation possible.

Internal Conflict

We tend to think of conflict as something happening *around us* or *to us*, but in reality, conflict is two-fold: that which comes from without, and that which comes from *within*. And inner conflict—which springs out of our intricate, complicated natures and resides within our hearts and minds—has just as much power and deserves at least as much consideration as the more straightforward external version.

Think of it this way: when direct light is blocked by an obstacle, a shadow is cast. So when you see your own shadow on a sidewalk—the obstacle causing it is you. We are often in our own way, even if we don't realize it. These internal shadows make up our "dark sides," the part of us that is chock-full of inner demons, fears, and negative traits that impede our progress. For you to turn conflict into triumph, these traits must be neutralized by being brought into the light of consciousness.

Internal conflict is often the biggest stumbling block that you will trip over on your way to fulfilling your quest. Therefore, you must identify the antagonist within yourself—you know, the one who feeds your inner fears about not being enough; the one who might move you to do things that you're not proud of or steers you toward a disingenuous, unhelpful action (or lack of action) that springs from a feeling of being unworthy or hopeless.

We've all heard of the angel and devil sitting on each of our shoulders. The angel whispers wise counsel and helps you make good decisions, while the devil—the "natural predator of the psyche" as described by author Clarissa Pinkola Estes—misleads and misdirects, fueling choices that create problems and hold you back. Your internal antagonist is basically the devil on your shoulder whose whispers are supposed to keep you safe from harm, but who really can keep you in neutral or send you in the wrong direction.

So, what happens when you are your own worst enemy? Pinpointing any patterns of self-sabotage is key.

The Four U's

Let's look back at your Protagonist Profile and take a closer look at the shadows that lurk within you using the four U-words:

Unearth. Find and mark your more unsavory traits or add them now if you didn't write any down before. Unearthing what you normally deny or repress will help you to accept your contradictions, ease your inner battles, and inch closer to your full, whole self.

Understand. Next, look at all your positive traits and ask yourself if there is a *downside* to that characteristic that also applies to you. For example, if you are ultra-organized, do you find it hard to be flexible? If you are sensitive to others, are you too sensitive to handle constructive criticism? If you are ambitious, do you feel threatened or envious if someone achieves before you do? To deepen your understanding, write these "shadow traits" down as well.

Unlock. Writers often invent a character who everyone loves to hate. Imagine yourself with *only* negative traits. Now, *Authorize It!* and plot out how this Grinch-like character's villainous side begins to soften through different experiences that let in the good so they can evolve. Does this character help someone? Do they do something uncharacteristically kind and get noticed? What other plot twists can help to embed positive traits? This reverse exercise is a step toward unlocking, owning, and transforming any negatives that appear in your profile. Once you've envisioned ways that a totally extreme character can transform, you can start to apply them to your own life, especially at work.

Unravel. Your identity has been molded by the stories you attached to your experiences, so be on the lookout for those hidden stories that you tell yourself and are not helping you on your quest. We often self-protect with stories that justify our actions or experiences, but much of what we whisper in our own ears is only partially true at best, or at worst, a lie. For years, I believed that my goddess-like mother was perfect and that I could only earn her love by looking and being more like her. But when I wrote my memoir, I saw her for who she truly was—a remarkable but also flawed woman whose remoteness was never my fault. So how can you unravel what's fiction and what's reality? Byron Katie's seminal book, *The Work*, offers four simple questions to dig deep and uproot any limiting belief:

1) *Is it true?*
2) *Can you absolutely know it's true?*
3) *How do you react, what happens, when you believe that thought?*
4) *Who would you be without that thought?*

All our inner conflict exploration so far will help you to rewrite any stories you're carrying for the better so that they loosen their grip and don't entirely block your progress.

Facing Conflict

At work, conflict flows through everything like a mighty river. Broader situations like mergers and acquisitions, management shake-ups, and marketplace shifts are often easier to handle in some respects because you are navigating them with everyone else in your sphere. In contrast, one-on-one conflicts can be much harder. The storylines here are endless, from sensing that there is tension with a co-worker, to suddenly finding yourself in a too-heated exchange. Maybe you and your boss have a major difference in opinion, or your subordinate challenged her annual review, or your boss's criticism in your own review shifted the dynamics in your relationship.

For any challenge or obstacle that you face, you will need to take action both externally—to confront and mediate the forces attempting to thwart you—*and* internally, to ensure that you address conflict in a way that moves you forward on your Character Arc. Here are four writerly conflict-resolving tips to help you *authorize* how you face your own shadows and deal with those that belong to others:

Tip #1: DIFFUSE & DISARM

In the heat of the moment—whether the conflict you're dealing with is external or internal—your first priority is to stop it in its tracks like a character cutting the wires of a timebomb. Whether it's a major blow-up with your antagonist or a more subtle thousand-paper-cuts situation, your goal is to deescalate. It is exceedingly difficult to reason with an unreasonable person (or with the unreasonable side of yourself), so try these tactics to mitigate the damage:

- **For an External Antagonist.** No matter how upset or hurt you are, stay calm, respectful, and poker-faced. Listen intently and take it all in without being defensive to demonstrate strength and quicken the end of the other person's venting. Try to control when and how the confrontation begins and ends. If you are caught off guard, attempt to set another time to discuss the issue so you can gather your thoughts. Then, when the intensity of the moment has passed, meet the issue head-on, acknowledge the tension, and probe for more context. Try to stay in dialogue-mode rather than debating the issue. Ask for their suggestion on what they think could help and offer any suggestions of your own. The ideal is to end with at least one positive, forward-looking solution.

- **For Your Internal Antagonist.** When you feel self-flagellation coming on, turn to Carl Jung and his "active imagination" process that can help you link to your unconscious while awake. Visualize what your inner critic looks like and ask it a series of direct questions like: *Why do you look the way you do? Why would you say that to me? What are you really trying to tell me?* Listen carefully to your first responses, then look straight into your inner critic's eye and say, *Thank you, but I choose not to listen.* To further press pause on the inner voice judging you harshly, apply the Unearth-Understand-Unlock-Unravel exercise to see if there is a different story angle that could ease the internal struggle.

Tip #2: DISCERN

Like a writer creating backstories and motivations for their different characters, try to figure out what the real issue is behind the conflict, and what your antagonist is trying to achieve.

- **For an External Antagonist.** Turn on your uber-observation skills and scan for non-verbal clues since body language can reveal ongoing insights. Are their arms crossed and blocking you? Are they nodding quickly to get the conversation over with? Are they avoiding direct eye contact? If yes, they could be disinterested or even deceitful. And, on the verbal side, if your antagonist intentionally or unintentionally reveals a vulnerability—say a fear or worry that they hold—really ponder it. If and when the time feels right, find a way to weave it back into a conversation. You might ask if they could tell you more about it while adding something that you're comfortable sharing about yourself. Deeper communication can break down barriers and might create a bridge between the two of you where none existed before.

- **For Your Internal Antagonist.** Major spirals can happen if one of your sore spots is triggered, sometimes by an incident that is entirely unrelated or innocuous. Harriet Lerner, Ph.D. and author of *The Dance of Anger*, notes that "We all come into relationships with hot-button issues from our own past. For one person it might be difficult dealing with someone who is judgmental. For another, it might be a person who treats you as if you're invisible." When your inner antagonist goes into overdrive at work, recognize that your reaction may be rooted in a deeper, unconnected issue. To separate the old baggage from the here-and-now—and to respond to the imminent conflict appropriately—pay attention to your sudden flares of anger or sadness, and to your body's non-verbal signals like sleeplessness, back pain, or stomach issues. Try to determine the source of your anxiety: *What am I really feeling? What does this feeling remind me of? What from my past am I still trying to heal?*

Tip #3: DETACH

A protagonist's emotions add dimension to the story, just as your feelings add depth to yours. But at work, there is a fine balance between the emotional and the rational, as well as the balance between the needs of the individual with the greater good. What's often required is emotional *distance* so that you can take in the bigger picture objectively—get an author's eye view of your conflicts—and then detach emotionally so you can respond to each foe with laser-like precision.

- **For an External Antagonist.** Think about your antagonist's character traits to figure out a strategy for resolving conflict. Here are a few common ones to get you started:
  - **The Narcissist:** Everything is about them. They are easily offended and can never be proven wrong. So skip over any blame when trying to resolve a problem (and if you want to get on their good side, compliment them and ask for advice).

71

- **The Passive-Aggressive:** They will side-step clear communication and then obstruct the process. This type subverts their frustrations to avoid conflict, so to best handle it with them, never criticize, keep your facial expressions neutral, and avoid revisiting their past mistakes.
- **The Martyr.** These ever-suffering types take on too much and then wallow in their sacrifices. To handle an issue, don't offer a solution that they'll just resist. Instead, acknowledge their hard work, ask how they feel and if there is something you can do to lighten their load.
- **For Your Internal Antagonist.** If you are too emotionally attached to your job, it can become your identity which, in turn, can make any conflict feel paralyzing. Hard work is absolutely necessary, obsessive work is not, so ponder if you might be too emotionally invested. When there is some work conflict, do you spiral downward full of anxiety? Do you often feel overwhelmed but afraid to set boundaries? Do confrontations make you feel as if your job will disappear and you'll be left with nothing? If you answer yes to any of these questions, your inner antagonist might be at work. Detach a bit by relaxing into something new (any interesting hobby will do), by establishing only one evening check-in time, and by building non-work relationships.

Conflict Epilogue

After the conflict resolves, find a trusted person to give you feedback about the situation and reality-check your views just like a writer getting feedback from an editor. A trusted mentor or colleague who also knows the antagonist can be especially helpful. Whatever the drama, it takes two to tango, so be open to honest feedback about how you may be playing a role.

Because our own fears and insecurities can make us unreliable narrators, it's common for us to circumvent our culpability by weaving a story that puts us entirely in the right and the other person squarely in the wrong—but as we've learned, this may not be correct. Writers purposely give their characters emotional blind spots to keep things interesting. Even as the H, you almost certainly have one that is obstructed from your view. So at work, it's important to discover what yours are or the confusion they cause will keep tripping you up. Blind spots manifest when we shut-out experiences or feelings that we find uncomfortable. Since awareness is key, start by simply asking: *What am I missing about myself or my actions? Do I keep having the same type of conflict over and over?* Think about three things that keep on happening to you no matter where you work or who you work with.

Once you see what you couldn't before, you'll have an easier time resolving conflict or stopping it from starting. So listen to the other person's feedback without judgment or defensiveness and, as you go forward, see where you might be able to compromise—without compromising your integrity—to untangle conflicts and make them work for you.

At Your Desk

Acknowledging conflict is one thing, mediating it as described above is another, and seeking to transform it for good is the holy grail. Doing so is an art form, and I want you to artfully, think like a writer and win.

A creative approach will allow you to more effectively deal with the top four external stressors that drive office conflict—**Competition, Challenge, Contradiction,** and **Criticism**—in a way that sparks positive change. Here are some writerly rules for deftly handling and transforming these obstacles into progress for you:

Rule #1: DON'T BE TOO SENSITIVE

Dealing with conflict calls for directness—and boldness. You are an H, after all. And because H's are always *for something* and not simply *against something*, they continually move towards fulfilling their quests with positive action. Like it or not, this requires them to be resourceful, proactive, and bold.

It's not always easy to be bold, however, especially when you have a sensitive underbelly. Sometimes, work can feel like *Survivor* meets *Mean Girls* meets *The Office*. As the H, you need to get tougher by not letting your sensitivities get the better of you. All companies have their own mission and everyone who works there is on their own journey with their own agenda. So when they do something that upsets you, it truly is more about them. Whatever is happening, learn from it and keep one enduring rule in mind: *never take it personally*. If you do, it will hijack your H's journey every time.

This sort of emotional immunity might seem unrealistic because often things don't simply *feel* personal—they *are* personal. The colleague who undermines the project you've been spearheading, the direct report who's been whispering behind your back, the peer who questions your competency —all of their arrows are directed straight at your heart. Still, if you lose sight of the fact that their behavior stems from their insecurities or desire to control *who you are*, you are giving them power over you. Instead, try to emotionally distance yourself by adopting a writer's observer POV to learn what you can (there might be some aspect that you do need to ponder). But don't take it personally. Doing so is akin to handing your narrative over to someone else.

So, no matter what happens, be sure that you define yourself despite what others say or do. Don't wither. Pick yourself up and march boldly forward. Just keep thinking of your adversaries as characters who are trying to "right" their own stories. You can't change them, so best not to let any toxicity from them penetrate you or sap your forward-motion energy.

And because it's sometimes more comfortable for sensitive types to lean back and vent about what's wrong rather than risk taking action to make things better, be sure to keep any pessimism in check. The gloomy character who stays mired in the worst parts of the day will inevitably accomplish little unless they do an about-face. While you always want to be honest about the realities you face at work, a fatalistic mindset won't make you a winner. Not only will it stymie growth by increasing your resistance to new solutions and opportunities, but management can pick up on such vibes in an instant and rarely rewards persistent naysayers.

Rule #2: PRIORITIZE

If I had to come up with a title that captures our current culture, I'd probably choose *Dazed & Confused: Why our 21st Century Society is Fractured, Distracted, and Overwhelmed.*

These days, it's hard to field all the priorities in your personal life, and often it's even harder at work. The responsibilities of the ever-on employee are as challenging as the demands of businesses that are chugging along 24/7—the thinning margins and smaller staff that most companies face can often make the tasks in a single day feel insurmountable—and technology creates as many problems as it solves. From Slack to DMs, emails to conference calls, to-do lists to texts, everything is coming at you every single second of your workday. How can you take control and decide what's important when it feels as if everything is?

Thinking like writers editing their drafts will help. In any evolving story, multiple characters, plotlines and sub-plots are competing for time and attention. The writer must decide which ones to focus on, and so must you. To do so, always recall your Narrative Arc and ask yourself:

- *What is the story I'm telling?*
- *What steps do I need to take to move that story forward?*

These two quest-centric questions can be used as a filter to help you concentrate on what matters most. Are you hoping to be chosen for the project team dedicated to your company's online presence? Then pursue anything related to social media dynamics and e-learning in the meantime. Are you working remotely and missing all the casual interactions that can propel careers forward, from friendly watercooler banter to the camaraderie of groups? Use your storytelling muscles to help you avoid being known or judged solely on what you produce—try signing on to Zoom calls five minutes early to engage in chit-chat or share an experience; build one-on-one relationships with private conversations that you initiate; start a virtual book club or happy hour to create opportunities for the whole you to shine through. Want to be sure that a raise is included with your next review? Start listing all your accomplishments now, with a tale about how each one has contributed to the company.

Keeping your Quotidian, Inventive, and Visionary action plans front-and-center will also help you to focus on the steps you need to take to reach your goal. Expend your energy appropriately and learn to set boundaries and deliverables so that you don't fly off-course. Oftentimes writers have to also say "No" to a passage or scene they love for the story's sake—they call this "killed darlings"—so use this editing mindset to discard your excess and improve your story's overall progress.

Rule #3: BE PROFOUND

In *Hamlet*, Shakespeare wrote: "The play's the thing wherein I'll catch the conscience of the king." Great writers aim to provoke thought with their scenes and themes because they know that their profound words have the power to change hearts and minds. To writers, being profound means deep-diving to get at the truth of something rather than swimming in superficial waters. And it also means to then articulate what they believe with clarity.

To be profound, you need to develop the same two talents:

- **A philosophical perspective** built upon your curiosity, objectivity, and independent thinking. Your goals: always seek substance over just scratching the surface *and* always avoid the lure of what everyone else is saying or doing. As a substantive person, your views will be heeded more readily, which helps you to overcome conflict and get ahead.
- **A communication style** that engages others and earns you respect for your ideas. Your most important insights can fall flat if they are not conveyed compellingly. By being an effective communicator,

you'll be better able to convince others that your way forward is the best way.

How to cultivate profundity and blossom into your most significant self at work despite inevitable conflict? Well, by its very definition, profundity means wisdom—and its many synonyms range from sophistication and astuteness, to brains and enlightenment—so it goes without saying that if you are all those things, you'll have an easier time facing down anything.

Shortcuts

Since many of the words that describe a profound character are born from experience and life's trial and error, let's *authorize* our path to becoming more profound with a few shortcuts:

Be a provocateur. Adopt a few qualities of the Trickster archetype that Campbell identified. Shake things up a bit with provocative open-ended questions that always lead you to more profound answers. As a coach, I learned that the most profound question you can ask anyone is, "Tell me about____." Asking someone to tell you more about their perspective on anything allows you to better understand them and their problems through information you wouldn't otherwise have. Closed questions, on the other hand, can usually be answered with a simple yes or no, which often leads nowhere. Authors understand the power of open-ended questions first-hand. When writing dialogue to move their stories forward, having characters ask closed questions that yield short, non-revealing responses—*Did you have fun? Are you happy?*—don't add dimension to the story. And questions like Why? can also be unproductive because they put characters on the defensive. Asking a person Why? can feel accusatory, like a judgment on the past in a way, and therefore opens the door to more conflict. But having their H frame open-ended questions that begin with, "Tell me," or "What, or "How" leads to deeper, more revealing dialogue that advances the story for the reader or viewer. At work, just keep asking provocative questions to discover the information you need so you can profoundly impact your solutions and results.

Stay open to possibility. Author Seth Godin took the inherent conflict within any new idea to its most profound level when he said, "The two opposing thoughts are: 'This might work' and 'This might not work.'" It's a freeing sentiment that keeps you open to possibility because no one ever knows how the story will end. There's always a way forward, so hold tight to possibility through open-ended questions like *What do you need to make this work?* to up your profundity quotient. You will surely benefit from unexpected answers that will inform your actions.

Get out of your comfort zone. Because wrestling with the new births the most interesting options, writers take protagonists out of their insular bubbles. Yet when left to our own devices, we all tend to stick with people who validate our beliefs because it's more comfortable. So, at work break out of your bubble and get into conversations with people from different departments who may hold viewpoints that oppose your own. Ask them about their perspective and listen. They may help you see something a new way and become more profound in the process—and may one day emerge as an ally.

Rule #4: KNOW YOUR REALITY

In the same way that we tend to seek the comfort of the familiar, we also tend to downplay or rationalize conflict. You may dislike much about your job but remain in it year after year because it allows you to work from home frequently. Similarly, you may know your role is not really suited to your talents, but you justify staying because leaving seems too daunting and overwhelming—or because deep down inside you hold limiting beliefs that whisper you're lucky to even have your current job.

To move toward a new vision, you must clearly grasp what you're moving away from by tossing any rose-colored glasses. This means staring conflict in the face and getting absolutely real. You want to:

- **Notice.** As objectively as possible, try to assess things as they are, with all the good and the bad. This is harder than it sounds because your personal backstory can influence and distort your own perspective—which is really *your* reality, not necessarily *reality as it is.* To best address this inherent conflict, you can try to:
    - Dispel any illusions you may have by reflecting and by accepting that *you may not be right*—someone else may have a more accurate POV.
    - Reality-check your views through continuous curiosity. This does not mean second-guessing your decisions, rather it means getting to the best-considered decisions in the first place because you've done the advance exploration.
    - Stay flexible by remembering that our Narrative and Character Arc cycles are akin to seasons we need to be ready for. This helps us to operate from a position of strength and agility as we field any unwanted realities that will come our way.
- **Contextualize.** *Before* developing any solutions be sure you understand what the real problem is. As you navigate your workplace realities to get the context around the problem and uncover its root cause, you first need the historical backstory:
    - Use the "Tell me more about" open-ended line of questioning to understand why things are the way they are.
    - Be sure to also dig for how the same challenge or a similar one was fielded before—and what happened. And revisit approaches or solutions that were once rejected or dismissed as not being effective enough. Sometimes a reveal comes too early in a story, and sometimes ideas are ahead of their time. Can something from the past be edited in a new way to solve the problem now?

When you've gathered your answers, not only will you be more informed, but you won't waste time repeating old plotlines (or suffer being dismissed with the "We've done this before" line). Figuring out the problem first always puts you in a better position to generate the right solutions.

- **Experience.** Characters always fumble around a new environment until they grasp what's going on. Although every job comes with an employee handbook, to fumble less often you must learn a company's *unwritten* rules by living them—not paying close attention to the reality of social codes and norms will waylay you every time. There usually is a chasm between a company's ideal culture and the reality of how people really behave. Your employee handbook may detail a flexible work policy, but the unwritten rule in your department might be to never arrive late or leave early. Just as a character's actions will speak louder than his words, tune into your company's real expectations—and to your co-worker's behavior—so something unexpected doesn't take you down.

Rule #5: PLOT YOUR MOVES

When you understand your realities and how to transform the conflict that you'll face on your quest, you'll be on your way to moving your story forward (and in an ideal world, your company's and your co-workers' stories as well).

To determine which path to take or what to try next, plot your own risks and rewards, just as an author who is weighing different scenarios does. Almost any writer's office is plastered with colored sticky-notes of all sizes, index cards galore, and erasable whiteboards. These necessary tools help to invent a new reality, plot scenes, create new possibilities, and monitor consequences to get to the ending they want.

So use the tool you're comfortable with to storyboard the scenes of whatever career vision you have. Then, as you evaluate the options, ask yourself:

- *Why do I want to do this?*
- *If I do this, what are the conflicts that I will face?*

80

- *If I do this, what are some intended and unintended consequences for me?*
- *What's the worst thing that could happen, and can I live with that?*
- *If I don't do this, what will happen, and can I live with that?*

Weighing your options through self-inquiry works just like a business decision matrix or scenario model. As you narrow down your choices, *authorizing* how you plot your moves will help you get to the considered decision that you're most comfortable moving forward with

Prompts

Ponder. Revisit Lesson Two's *What's My Story?* Narrative Arc depiction of how you lived through the four cycles of a particular incident, what you felt, and how you acted and reacted. Now, extend another line from each of the four parts and write down the *specific obstacles you faced* during each cycle (conflicts can be internal, interpersonal, or external). Time for more self-inquiry: *How did I move past or around each obstacle I faced? Is there anything I wish I had done differently? What were some of the successful ways I overcame the conflicts that I can now own as part of who I am? Is there something I wish I had done or handled differently?*

Probe. With what you think your quest might be in mind, make a list of the potential conflicts or obstacles that stand in the way of fulfilling that quest. Add a second column that reframes each challenge into a positive to overcome the barrier (i.e.: Reframe limited time into the option of waking up an hour earlier each day; turn strained financial resources into the possibility of a partnership or collaboration to share costs).

Probe. Many believe that conflicts in our dreams are the literal expressions of our inner, subconscious battles. Write down any such dreams that you recall, especially recurring ones, or dreams where you are the aggressor, or where you fall, or can't do something you used to do. Look for clues to indicate what you might be really fighting against.

Map. Make two columns—Proactive and Reactive—and categorize people at work who are one or the other. Next to each of their names in the appropriate column, list one strength, one weakness, and one conflict you've seen them overcome. Any patterns? Which column is ultimately more successful? Then circle only your antagonist(s). Ask: *What can I learn from them? How can I detach to view them and the conflict they cause differently?*

Identify. What are your most important interpersonal skills that can help you effectively deal with conflict? Also, name some of your traits that may hinder resolving a challenge or confrontation. What can you work on to improve?

Identify. Pick a person who is a good mediator. Ask them to help you role-play to solve a conflict you're facing but have been avoiding because you don't want to confront it. Then summon the courage to have the conversation you've been sidestepping in a friendly, productive way. As an icebreaker, ask them to tell you more about their perspective on something unrelated, and see if the conversation opens up any interesting talking points.

Imagine. Building on your *What's My Company's Story?* answers, what are the biggest marketplace obstacles your company is facing? Also name the biggest obstacles your customers, clients, and partners are facing. Compare and contrast them to find their commonalities and differences. Are there any insights from how you personally maneuvered around an obstacle that could be applied to your company? Then think about your company's quest and write down any realities of how the business is run that stand in the way of fulfilling their mission. From siloed departments to competing agendas, list the inner conflicts that may be in the way to deepen your own understanding.

Authorize It! Live

Lesson Three

"I'm a project manager at a pretty progressive tech company that tries to instill a strong corporate culture. Our values are written all over the walls, our mission is clear and so are our objectives; we have meditation rooms, all-hands meetings, free food, and an end-of-day happy hour once a week. But we've grown a lot and many things that are supposed to get done just don't. People seem to want to avoid working as much as possible and resist being held accountable. In group meetings, everybody says "Yes," but now I understand what a "pocket veto" means—when they leave the room or hang-up the remote call, they just put it aside and don't do much of anything. This makes my job incredibly frustrating, and I feel as if I always have to chase everything down. I think I'm becoming everyone's worst nightmare. Help!"
Kate

Kate, although there are always stellar superstars in any office, every manager also has to deal with inertia and those who wish to skate by with minimum effort, or who get so used to the perks that they feel entitled instead of grateful. A lot of this is just human nature.

Especially within modern companies that aspire to a set of values, the employees that are drawn to it can have an idealized view of their own virtuousness and talents, which makes these shadow traits even trickier to handle. Human nature being what it is, the only thing that you can control is your response to this conflict between your quest and the behavior of everyone else.

Project managers like yourself are usually super-organized, detail-oriented task-masters. Rather than doing the specific work on the project, they are responsible for making sure everyone else does. So, there's an innate conflict between the point person that is you and those you need to herd that's automatically built into your role. If workloads increase and people are not cooperating, your natural skills and tendencies may be heightened to a negative level that only serves to push people further away.

In today's transparent and sensitive workspaces, you need to strike a delicate balance. In my corporate heyday, if I didn't do what I was supposed to do, my boss would snap: "Just do your job," with the implication that if I didn't figure it out and do it, I would be fired. That doesn't cut it today. So, to help transform this adversarial situation, I recommend the following:

Detach. Step back and see this for what it is as non-emotionally as you can. Taking it personally would only serve to sabotage your progress.

Discern. When you're not chasing people down for something, seek their input. You need to build a feedback loop with those around you so that you can better understand them and their specific work habits and needs (or at least act as if you do). And you need to break down their defensiveness. Like teenagers whose mother is checking up, they may resent your role, or feel that your job is the easy one—they're doing all the work and you're just checking off boxes on a project management tool. So, try to understand your characters and the challenges they face. Ask them: What's the hardest part of the work you do? What's one thing you wish you could change? Where are the sticking points with this project? *Tell me one thing I can do for you or I need to know.* With active listening, you'll be learning, deepening relationships with your co-workers, and maybe even discovering better ways to complete projects.

An H Check-in. With your own evolution in mind, ask yourself about how you can best respond to the push-back you face if you want to grow. Also think about how these recurring flare-ups might be evolving you in negative ways, like becoming uncharacteristically irate in your attempt to do your job well or becoming someone who doesn't feel like the real you. Ask yourself what you need to change or let go of to stop that from happening.

Plot Your Moves. Once you gather information from people, come up with a solution that might improve overall outcomes, and then proactively take a recommendation to your boss and/or management. With all the benefits your company has in place already, perhaps one is missing— rewards. Whether monetary or recognition-based, people are more motivated when they are chasing a goal with intermittent incentives. Do your research online, gather supporting data, and then suggest connecting performance to tangible rewards and you'll make your job easier, your colleagues grateful, and your company's story (and yours!) better.

A Follow-Up with Sharon from Chapter One:

Sharon, as you grapple with finding your passion and your quest, it's possible that inner conflict may be your biggest obstacle. The people around you who appear to be so together and successful may be different from you in one key way: they don't pay as much attention to the devil on their shoulder as you do.

So, ask yourself Byron Katie's four questions to determine if negative whispers are affecting your self-esteem. Do you feel that you are incapable of rising through the ranks to a position you'd enjoy? Are you just as reluctant to branch out and create something on your own? Do you believe that you don't have the talent or the ability to withstand the humiliation if it doesn't work out?

To overcome these private fears, plot your possible moves and outcomes, including the worst-case scenario. Suppose you did try something, and your first attempt crashed and burned. How could you weave that adventure into your personal story in a positive way?

Also, it's time to let go of pessimism and sensitivity. From daily affirmations that underscore your new mantra of not taking things personally, to glass-half-full instead of half-empty thoughts, try to keep an H's mindset. Reviewing the internal antagonist tips in the four D's and getting feedback from someone you trust can also help you paint a clearer portrait of yourself and what some of your next steps could be.

Even if you are not having any outward conflicts at this time, it's possible that envy or even resentment might creep in and impact your relationships with friends and people at the office. Pay attention to how your behavior might rile someone or make them feel as if you just don't care. Do your best to prevent this from happening—whatever form your quest ultimately takes, it will be easier with allies.

Lesson Four: Seek the Unconventional

A storyline has to be unpredictable and sometimes even counterintuitive to be interesting. *Scream*'s classic opening scene inverts expectations by killing off the movie's biggest star—Drew Barrymore—in the first few minutes. *Game of Thrones* is notorious for shocking twists and dispensing with seemingly indispensable characters. And the tenth-anniversary release of the bestselling *Twilight* series, *Life and Death*, turns the tables and tells the same forbidden love story differently by switching the genders of vampire Edward and mortal Bella. In all these tales, the conventional is out the window, all bets are off, and no one knows what's coming next.

This storytelling truth is essential for you to keep in mind as you move forward on your quest. Ironically, despite living in a data-driven, analytical, immediate (and what should therefore be a more predictable) age, answers are often more elusive and erratic than they have ever been. So, while you can still turn over your tried-and-true "rocks" when looking for work solutions, the world is accelerating so quickly and technology is changing how we live so dramatically that the familiar or historically significant is *no longer enough*. Returning to methods that worked in the past can be a starting point, but today we all should look under unfamiliar rocks as well.

We are all wired to seek patterns because we equate understanding with safety. But new ground cannot be gained, and new problems cannot be solved just by doing the same old things. Why? Because the only way to guarantee a different conclusion is to change things up by seeking the unconventional. And that applies equally to how you contribute at work *and* how you live out your personal story.

When I was leading magazine brands, every client wanted a "big idea." With each one, my team and I didn't think there would ever be another. Once, we were completely out of ways to transform *Metropolitan Home* from the underdog magazine it was to a category leader. Until we approached our annual showhouse—a home that many "shelter" magazines transform with well-known interior designers and brand sponsors—unconventionally. Even though we were mired in doubt, our marketing team created a partnership with the Showtime network and then brought on interior designers to create a new kind of showhouse, one with rooms inspired by Showtime's hit series like *The Tudors*, *Dexter*, *Californication*, *The L Word*, and *Weeds*. It broke all the rules of more staid, traditional showhouses and we were uncertain about how it would be received by our industry. But it was a hit; a breakthrough collaboration that brought *Metropolitan Home* powerful awareness and made the magazine as fascinating as the most compelling H. Suddenly, clients who had stopped returning our calls now clamored to join us in whatever we would be dreaming up next. One atypical creative solution garnered millions of media impressions, won awards, and brought us new respect, authority, and revenue.

Writers instinctively know the power of the unexpected and guide their characters accordingly. The H starts to change and grow only after their normal world is interrupted and they're thrown into unfamiliar waters. Slowly they learn to experiment and trust that their instincts will get them to a better place—and you must do the same.

Seeking the unconventional will help you arrive at that better place. The unconventional turns things around, opens new doors, and delivers the surprising discoveries that amp-up success. So search for unpredictable and unexpected answers everywhere around you and commit to doing things differently than you've done before.

Sometimes the easiest way to uncover the new is to let go of what no longer serves. Some tightly held notions in your work world may be part of an old story, or a storyline that started out as true might have reached its natural conclusion. The same is true in Character Arcs. H's transform by letting go of, or changing their relationship to, the past. Let the ideas and sparks and hopes that are floating like bubbles inside of you rise and fly off in entirely new directions. Even if this seems daunting, remember that as the H, you can make it happen.

Flip the Switch

The counterintuitive new strategies or non-traditional results that you're seeking are often ones that are contrary to what *should be* true but nevertheless *are true*. To discover the unconventional, you will need to practice seeing things a different way. To do this, try the following:

Picture being underwater and opening your eyes to a completely different world.

Stand on your head or try an inversion table for an entirely different view.

Turn an image upside down to shift your perspective.

Say *perhaps*. Answer any question with this simple word to leave room for possibility.

Ask *What if* **and** *Why not?* After asking revealing open-ended questions to ground you, get to unconventional and stunning results by asking these two little but powerful queries. *What if?* kicks your imagination into overdrive, and *Why not?* liberates you to take action. In *Once Upon a Time in Hollywood*, writer and director Quentin Tarantino asked himself the same two questions as he rewrote the true story of the 1969 Manson murders into an unexpected fairy tale ending and won one hundred twenty-nine awards in the process.

Reverse your thinking. In the writing world, there are "Pantsers" and "Planners." Pantsers literally fly by the seat of their pants and go with the flow of the story they are writing without an outline, and planners map the entire story out in advance. Whatever your typical style is, flip it to see where the opposite approach may take you.

Play this-meets-that. This game can be a way to stimulate new ideas, in the same way my book, *Saturday's Child*, was described as *"Dirty Dancing* meets *Goodfellas."* You may not know exactly what it's about from that description, but you have a definite sense in just a few words. Use it when you're working on a new product—*It's **this** meets **that***—or when you're thinking about who you're aspiring to be—*I want to be **this** H meets **that** H*—from your favorite books, series, or films.

To complement your new unconventional mindset, you can continue to see things differently by remembering that there is always more to the story and life is rarely one hundred percent right or one hundred percent wrong, all-or-nothing, or either-or. Writers understand this and drift toward the more complex middle ground—what could be a little of two choices or even neither choice—to make a story more interesting. And it is in this middle where the best solutions you need for work await.

Because it's simpler to think in an either-or way—*if you're this, then you must be that*—we tend to view things conventionally and without the nuances that tell the whole story. An either-or mindset—what I call *Ordinary-think*—allows you to choose between two mutually-exclusive things and then to move forward with one. But when we go there as our first resort, we cut ourselves off from the full spectrum of unconventional possibilities.

Extraordinary-think, on the other hand—the ability to create and hold a constellation of simultaneous ideas—is what we need to do before so we can first develop the possibilities that will be narrowed down later.

The secret sauce is in the *balance and order* of the two ways of thinking. Always understand the problem that you are solving first, come up with a multitude of new ideas second, and then as your third step, narrow down to two choices and decide. And, after you whittle to an either-or choice, continue to think like a writer and consider if there is an alternative answer—a sub-plot in a way—that may be found in the middle ground between the two choices.

Lights On!

Imagine that your agency is on the hunt for a new client and your bosses put the need for new revenue on your shoulders. Here's how to approach the situation unconventionally for better results:

Dig to understand the real problem. It's not just that the agency has been struggling with revenue for over a year because it lost three of its top clients. The departing accounts were all from the same depressed industry the agency specializes in. However, this bleak outlook has not been addressed.

Re-state the problem to make it quest-centric. Win a new client from a *growing category* to *expand our expertise* and increase revenue now and in the future.

Discovery phase. All marketplace trends point to the Health & Wellness category, and within that general space, appliances used to prepare nutritional shakes are the best fit for the agency. The question: "Should we choose to pitch the leading Nutribullet brand or another blender brand?" Now, see how different the answers are if we go to ordinary-think before rather than after developing possibilities.

Ordinary-think answer: Health and Wellness trends point to increasing awareness for the leading Nutribullet brand so we should pursue them.

Extraordinary-think answer: Health and wellness trends, underlying demographics, and projected growth trajectory establish this category as the one to focus on. Within it, there is increasing awareness for

Nutribullet, which will heighten general demand for nutritious shakes at-home. This will increase market-share for all blenders, especially as traditional blender brands begin to market their shake capabilities and recipes. The winner will be the one who best engages the consumer, so our go-forward choice is to pursue one of the other legacy brands who need our help to compete with Nutribullet and capture their share of the wellness market. Success with a competitive brand will also open the door for us to work with new products and services like Daily Harvest's delivery of pre-packaged shake ingredients for any available appliance.

The Art of Transformation

There is a well-known truism about innovation: The car is not the horse-and-buggy plus ten percent. Yes, both are transportation, but a car is not an *incremental* gain over the buggy. It is a *leap*, a whole new way of getting from point A to point B.

As a child, my favorite activity was connect-the-dots books, so I had an *aha* moment when I read that Apple Founder Steve Jobs said, "Creativity is just connecting things." Some connections are obvious—it's the not-so-obvious unconventional ones that you're after. Connecting disparate things —in effect, doing a mash-up—leads to new ideas, just like cross-pollination breeds new plants and flowers. The same kind of cross-category, lateral, out-of-the-box thinking is crucial if you want to make progress on your quest. An inspired hiker, looking closely at what made burrs stick to his clothing, ultimately invented Velcro. Likewise, you must drop the barrier of preconceived notions so you can open up to what could be possible.

It is a standard business practice to mash-up dissimilar, disconnected, adjacent ideas when inventing something new. Award-winning design firm IDEO's pairings of odd, unexpected things always spark fresh ideas—one of their recent mashups of hospitals and hotels yielded clever mini-bars filled with healthy snacks in patient's rooms. When I was running innovation teams on the hunt for the next big thing, playing mash-up was the path to a new story. Multi-colored Post-it notes and whiteboards were everywhere as we mixed-and-matched the ideas and trends we had discovered in sync with our company's strengths and expertise. Forced associations between music and fashion, cars and design, pets and home, and wellness and family yielded new products we could launch and big bold ideas that we could sell.

Early on, before I was even in corporate marketing or innovation, I was gobsmacked by an idea after watching a splashy new Virgin Atlantic commercial, followed by a separate one for Virgin Records. It suddenly dawned on me that Virgin's two largest markets were likely the same as my publishing company—the U.S. and the U.K.—and that perhaps we could combine forces to create an American-British initiative. I learned that the twenty-fifth anniversary of The Beatles landing on our shores was coming up and thought, *What if?* we could invent a retrospective promotion that united air travel between the two countries with music and our fashion brands?

Even though it was not my territory, I then thought *Why not?* and moved forward. I drafted a simple one-sheet outlining a marketing idea that Virgin could sponsor as a new advertiser in our magazines and, with my boss's permission, I showed it to the right internal person. He was intrigued, especially because my no-risk proposal—I offered to do all the work myself and close the deal on my own time—made it so easy for him to say yes. At the very least, it would spur some new thinking and relationships (and at the very best, lots of new revenue), so he agreed. I ran with it and gave it my all, and even though we came oh-so-close, it ultimately did not sell. But what unconventionally seeking new territory did do was advance my career. Management saw me differently after that moment and it paved the path for my future roles in marketing, international sales, and ultimately, innovation.

You can leverage the unconventional by using five bold, perspective-changing writerly techniques:

Technique #1: BORROW BRILLIANCE

Great writers immerse themselves in the words of other authors. Breathing in masterful expression keeps them on their toes and allows them to "borrow brilliance" as they are inspired to play with new and unconventional styles that elevate their own work. In fact, writers never tire of discovering and discussing the words of other authors, just like Ernest Hemingway, Simone de Beauvoir, and F. Scott Fitzgerald debated literature in the cafes of Paris long ago. The same applies to the business world, and you should always "read" your competitors to figure out how they do what they do. It's a fact that you don't always need to reinvent the wheel—often you can morph an existing idea to work for your own objectives. After all, many stories share a common theme or plot and are simply retold with new characters and twists—think about the star-crossed lovers' theme, from *Romeo and Juliet* to *West Side Story* to hundreds of other well-known tales.

As you borrow brilliance from the best practices of other executives and brands, be sure to think unconventionally and study unrelated companies too—it gets especially interesting when they're not like you at all. Those different industries are likely solving a problem that is analogous to yours. All businesses offer a product or service and have manufacturing, distribution, and sales components. Whether it's Nike's latest celebrity-endorsed sneaker or Netflix's breakthrough in streaming programming, the efforts, successes, and setbacks of unrelated companies are all there for the borrowing and the tweaking. And you can also borrow from your personal life. Study what moves *you* to action. What do you scroll through and subscribe to and take screenshots of? What grabs your attention—or the attention of your friends—instantly?

Borrowing brilliance on your quest will help you to improve the story you're telling by:

- **Granting** you fresh trains of thought and insights that will heighten your creativity.
- **Identifying** you as a thought-provoking, bigger vision employee.
- **Informing** new strategies and tactics at the office that will be attributed to you.

Technique #2: SURPRISE

No one likes reading a novel or watching a movie where the ending is obvious, so every story requires an element of surprise to keep the reader or viewer engaged. But in a great tale, the unexpected ending makes perfect sense and, when you look back, you realize that it was there all along. It was "foreshadowed." The author had sprinkled little clues hinting at the surprise throughout—a breadcrumb trail of tiny reveals that set up what was to come —that you missed because they didn't seem important at the time. The ending of a suspense novel is usually a shock because often, it diverges totally from what you were expecting. Everyone is blown away at the end of *The Sixth Sense* when we realize that the character of Dr. Malcolm Crowe, played by Bruce Willis, is really dead—throughout the entire film, he was a ghost that only the preternatural boy could see.

In our digital era where moments are captured and reviewed in a split second, Polaroid pictures have made an unexpected resurgence, especially at parties. Author Annie Lamott believes that holding the iconic, white-bordered photograph as its image takes shape is akin to the charm and allure of the developing story; of the slow coming-into-focus that hints at what is to come. That is a stage-setting thought that speaks to the benefits of looking beyond what is readily apparent, and of following a counterintuitive trail at work. For example, on a quest to make their mass-market snacks healthier, PepsiCo sought unconventional guidance from high-end chefs because only they knew how to reduce salt and sugar and still yield a tasty product. It's the surprise twist that holds the answers you're chasing. Problems that need solving require a business as *unusual* mindset, so ask yourself: *What would surprise our customers or critics? What kind of pivot would seem unbelievable? Is there some shade of grey or nuance that can take my project up a notch?*

And remain confident that, like foreshadowing in a story, every single thing you have done before, every skill you have picked up along the way (even in those jobs that were supposedly meaningless or a waste of time), is there for a reason and will surprise you by coming back around to play a role. Think of opportunities like a Boggle game, with each talent of yours written on a cube and just waiting to be shaken out in an endless number of new combinations. Your skills are transferable to new roles and new industries, and embracing an unconventional mentality will help you find opportunities.

Technique #3: ANTICIPATE

Any H is the catalyst and mover of their story and is always active, never passive. Early on, they may be more reactive than proactive, but as they move along on their Narrative and Character Arcs, they step into their power. You too must take ownership of your story and be the force behind the unconventional thought propelling you forward—one way you can do that is by *anticipating what's next*.

Remember the swamp scene in *The Princess Bride?* The writer ratchets-up the suspense by presenting three seemingly insurmountable challenges that Buttercup and Westley must survive: "rodents of unusual size," fire spurts, and lightning sand. They do so by anticipating what is coming their way—once they learn how the sandpits are disguised and that a popping sound always precedes the fire, they can sidestep both. Then Westley applies this new knowledge while wrestling one of the terrifying rodents—the familiar pop-pop sound tells him exactly when to roll over toward the fire and he emerges victorious.

Just like those H's, part of your quest is to anticipate the sinkholes at the office. The saying, "Chance favors the prepared mind," speaks to the fact that there really aren't lucky people, only those who are primed and ready. The reward goes to the person who anticipates problems and works toward preventing them, and who is constantly taking in and assessing new information. Be in storyteller mode as if you are thinking ahead to the next chapter. What could happen here? What might go wrong? *How do I solve the problem?*

We tend to plan for success with any project but anticipating something that could go wrong along the way—and then taking small steps to prevent it in the first place—is smart business. Some might consider it pessimistic thinking, but it is actually a realistic contingency plan approach. It doesn't matter which HGTV show you watch, part of the storyline always involves dealing with the unexpected, and as walls come down and cabinets go up,

98

the problems that manifest along the way are solved with unconventional ideas. The hosts apply their expertise and perspective to prepare homeowners for what could be ahead, and then, after the challenges baked into each episode are vanquished, a magnificent result is revealed. In the same way, poke holes in your work story so you can anticipate the low points as well as the high to keep your next chapter on course.

And as you do, always remember that anticipating will also limit the unwanted surprises that you would otherwise face. To prevent any meeting from going astray, adopt a diplomatic mindset before the group discussion. Have individual prep calls in advance whenever possible so you can gauge and best align with what the other person needs and expects to ensure a happier ending.

Technique #4: TREND-SPOT

Reader's tastes ebb and flow, as do book genres. One year, it's all about historical fiction, and the next, thrillers or futuristic androids. Even if an author has written a story that out-Dracula's *Dracula*, if the current publishing marketplace has had its fill of vampires, the best book in the world about these charismatic bloodsuckers won't see the light of day.

Trends are waves of unconventionality that usher in something new. And all companies—and the products they create—thrive best when they are in sync with marketplace trends, and when they deliver a solution to an identified consumer problem or need. Trends can be accelerated by world events or cultural shifts like the 2020 pandemic, which led to silver linings like upgraded online learning and virtual connection, as well as more flexible work-from-home schedules.

According to *Tipping Point* author Malcolm Gladwell, trends are actually like viruses. There is a "patient zero" starting point, and then a broadening to early adopters, influencers, and connectors who spread the trend over time. Spotting trends *before* they reach their "tipping point" and spread like wildfire is a critical skill for both you and your company. When I was a chief innovation officer, I devoted twenty percent of my time to a "lab"—a team of six executives whose sole responsibility was to discern and develop future opportunities. Right before Apple unveiled the first iPhone that could flip the camera's perspective—an advancement that would birth selfies—the most prescient among our group said, "this feature will change everything." We immediately sensed he was right even if we could not fully envision then what was to come.

The excitement was limited to techies at first, but a hundred billion selfies later, the flip feature went well beyond just another cool camera function, adding a new word into the vernacular and becoming integrated into our daily lives. And those who saw its potential early—and created related opportunities around it, from vlogging sticks to social platforms—benefited the most. Success follows when you anticipate what consumers (or other businesses) need, and then transform what you do to deliver on that need in some way. Those are the big ideas that can change businesses and make you shine. So how can *you* make this happen? Two skills demand your attention and polishing: *research* and *data storytelling*.

Research to spot trends has never been easier—or more fun. Searching online for information that could potentially inform your quest and solve a problem is akin to a scavenger hunt. One result leads to another, and your macro and micro trend discoveries will reveal clues, a new promise, or an unseen opportunity. A few easy-to-access sources to get your ideas popping are Google's search trends, YouTube's trend dashboard, *BuzzFeed*'s content shares, *Trend Hunters'* industry predictions, *Sparks & Honey*'s daily culture briefings, and *Mashable*'s trend forecasts.

When you find something that piques your interest or has possible resonance with your industry, you will really need to think like a writer and be a data storyteller. You must be able to interpret the data and turn it into a story so other people can easily grasp its potential. Just as writers do with their books and screenplays, you need to make sense of the complex through words and visuals so others can understand what they previously did not.

In the innovation lab that I was a part of, we discovered a powerful business need and had to stretch our data storytelling muscles. We realized that our fashion editors could use their cellphones' video recording functionality at runway shows, but the biggest frustration was creating a post-able highlights story with a beginning, middle, and an end from the content they captured. So we did a little extraordinary-thinking and narrowed down our choices. The winner was from our group's tech mastermind—we would create an App that streamlined the footage into a one-minute story template that could then be shared.

Through the story we spun from the research and data we uncovered, we convinced management that they needed to invest in this App's development—not only would be able to gather footage in real-time and build our editors' personas to the public, but we would lower costs because the editors could do it themselves and replace expensive camera crews and photo-sharing services.

After we launched it, we made an unexpected discovery—consumers also had the same frustration with sharing a video story of their child's football game or ballet recital. So we got back to work and in the days before Instagram was even dreamed of, we created the *Rec-This* story recording App with the ability to edit video into a shareable act one, two, and three—with background music! We told potential users a story—not about the analytics or the functionality, but about how it solved their problem and how much happier they would be with it rather than without it. We touched emotional chords by showing happy relatives receiving the one-minute videos, along with children looking back on their childhood highlights. The result? Ten out of ten stars in the App store at the time, and lots of cheering families.

So as you seek your own unconventional ideas, be sure to leverage the power of researching trends and data storytelling to propel your story forward.

Revise

We now know the importance of editing yourself and of even giving your company an EDIT. This mindset is especially important when you are building the story you're telling. Think of the books on a library shelf. Any one that you check-out is probably draft two hundred—before it hit the shelves, every word was finessed by an author whose mind was always spinning with unconventional new angles. Just as with writing, revisions are a key part of any creative process, project, or initiative at work. The power to iterate and to pivot; to reimagine entirely, or to discard in favor of a better, unexpected discovery along the way is always in your hands. So you should accept and welcome the constant process of finessing and tweaking, of assemblage and reassemblage, of necessary incremental gains to get to the breakthrough one (like that buggy and car).

This acceptance will help fuel a positive mindset for those dark, hard days when you feel like you're getting nowhere. If you're stuck, start by getting the first draft of an idea or solution that you want to pursue out of the air and on the page—know that it's going to be imperfect but that's just the way it is. Even if your early attempts are flat, each revision will improve your draft and can push you further outside the conventional box.

To sustain this editorial mindset of continuous improvement, ask yourself which statement you agree with: (A) You are born talented or not. (B) You can improve the talents you have. Almost all of us would say that the second is the truer statement—even if we don't believe it about ourselves, at least at first. One speaks to a fixed approach to life and the other to a flexible one. If every writer felt that their character was forever fixed in the same place, the story would go nowhere. So remember that everything you work on can be continually refined, and holding an unconventional mindset will ensure that each new version will be tighter and stronger.

Double Down on Your Strengths

These above techniques will spur the best unconventional ideas when you apply them to your inherent strengths and talents, and to areas where you excel. At work, your strongest attributes are also called core competencies—hard and soft skills that can range from leadership to organizational ability, decision-making to reliability—that combine to form a cogent profile of who you are. Hopefully, the Prompts and the Protagonist Profile have helped to identify yours because if you want to get ahead, you'll need to focus on becoming as masterful as possible where you excel. Putting effort toward improving your weaker areas is never a bad thing, but as you advance you can always delegate parts of the job that are not your strong suit to others or collaborate to overcome them. The key is to concentrate on continually improving what you're great at and then leveraging it to win.

These four writing-world methods for developing your strengths and using them to lead you to unconventional solutions will give you maximum advantage at the office:

Method #1: BE MISSION-DRIVEN

All writers demand that each chapter—every scene and every line—pays off and adds to the story that they're telling. Let that singular focus keep your quest and story moving forward. Your company will be (or should be) focused on the pursuit of opportunities aligned with its mission and values, and so must you.

True writers have the discipline to be mission-driven about putting a fine point on their talent every day, just as weavers weave and artists paint and musicians play. Even the most accomplished opera singers will rarely go a day without training and using their voice. So, no matter your expertise, you should approach your talents as a creator would and purposefully hone your "craft." Practice what you're good at, take online tutorials to expand your knowledge, sign-up for newsletters, join special interest groups to stay current in your strength areas, and follow influencers who share similar strengths and are on the cutting edge.

And just like sub-plots add dimension to the plot of a story, each one of your talents has different components and related skills that can be enhanced. If one of your talents is communication, you could study interviewing or active listening techniques so that you will be even more effective; if your talent is humor, you could study improvisation to relate to others even more. The newness you discover along the way will always expand your conventional understanding.

And finally, although authors can broaden to any category at any time, most writers have a specific genre that they specialize in. You too should be equally focused on the area where your expertise is the strongest to advance faster and command more.

Method #2: BE INGENIOUS

Success in almost any job boils down to coming up with unconventional solutions and then crafting the right stories about them at the right time in the right way. So as you double down on your strengths, also work twice as hard to develop those storytelling muscles of yours at work *every day*. One way you're going to build them, of course, is by reading this book through to the end. Another way is to regularly read—not just the stories that entertain us but those that instruct through the moral and ethical questions that they raise. Aesop's Fables are ingenious—and fun—examples, with each tale teaching a life lesson in a fantastical way. I could *tell* you: Be prepared. Or I could let you read *The Ant and The Grasshopper* and *show* you what happens when you're not. So, take a "business fables" approach and tell stories to prove your point. Add emotion to help people understand what they need to take-away, and include values and objectives where you can.

Method #3: BE IN CONVERSATION

In my years in magazines and brand innovation, I had become an expert at asking the right business questions—ones that focused on past performance as an indicator of the future. Whether it was determining if a prospective job candidate would be a good fit or if a potential business collaboration would work out, I believed that I had to draft *all* the questions in advance to be sure everything would be covered (and, in a way, to validate what I assumed was true after all my research and prep). In other words, my pre-conceived notions. In truth, I went into every session with the answers almost as formed in my mind as the questions were. Which meant that I was cutting myself off from new, unconventional thoughts.

When I entered the book publishing world, however, the experiences that I had on tour upended how I approach questioning, in the same way becoming a coach did. The hand-raisers in the audience didn't ask me easy "job interview-type" questions that looked backward at my performance history to predict the future. Rather, they asked open-ended *forward-looking* questions that I had to grapple with on the spot. "Tell us more about what made you so compelled to write this book? Could you have written this book if your mother had been alive? What does success look like for you now? What do you want readers to feel? What will you write next? Their expansive questions got me to in-the-moment, unexpected answers and gave them more revealing insights.

And each audience question seemed to prompt more *follow-up questions*. As I went even deeper, I realized that this is where the magic lies—in the follow-up, in the moment, *in conversation*. New, unconventional insights are born from these real-time exchanges and the drilled-down responses they elicit. Now, whenever I'm in a meeting or gathering information for a new project, I know that I don't need all the answers going in, and I certainly don't have to have all the questions because they will appear in real-time if you let curiosity drive your conversations.

This awareness is particularly powerful for H's who tend to hold themselves back at work or are overly cautious because they feel that if they don't know *all* the answers, they can't move forward. But the truth is that you don't need to know them, you just need to know *what* to ask and *how* to ask it in a way that will elicit the most information for you.

PLOT

Keep this writing acronym in mind for all your real-world dialogue and you'll set yourself up for success:

P = Probe for more with open-ended questions.

L = Live in the moment of the conversation, ready to follow-up and go deeper.

O = Opportunistic plotlines will appear as you listen to challenges and situations.

T = Twist the problems you hear into forward-looking actions and new possibilities.

Method #4: BE A MENTOR

Most writers freely offer guidance and advice to fellow writers, often serving as early readers or providing testimonial blurbs for new books and debut authors. In the process, not only do they strengthen what they already know by sharing it with someone else, they often pick-up an unconventional thought or new approach that could benefit their own work down the road. So whatever your expertise, spread it around freely. Whether with an intern, co-worker, or a friend, sharing your knowledge will further strengthen what you already know every time. And that will help you to advance and keep you open to an unconventional thought or two that you'll pick up in the conversation. Plus, extending a helping hand to someone else is its own reward—not only will you get internal gratification, but giving of yourself unconditionally always seems to find its way back around.

Prompts

Ponder. As you did with your *What's My Story?* incident where you lived through the four cycles, now do the same for the most unconventional, non-traditional—even totally uncharacteristic—thing you've ever done or taken a chance with. Break down that event by the four cycles—Shift, Instability, Darkness, Light—and note what happened in each. Ask yourself: *Did my leap result in learning that I now carry with me? Did the experience make me less cautious or more cautious? How did it change my attitude or outlook in some way?*

Non-traditional

Identify. Be a change-agent who is always looking for what's on the horizon and think about a problem your team is trying to solve. To get new insights, talk to end-users and co-workers in different departments. Take the problem up to its highest level (at 40,000 feet, is it really just about attracting more customers?) Then, explore entirely different industries. Can you apply anything they are doing to your scenario?

Probe. Is every single scene from your day paying it off in a mission-driven way? Focus is the keyword here. Think about your most recent full week at work. Were your actions each day singular in focus? How did they contribute to moving you forward in the way that you wanted? How did they further align your story with the overarching story of your company?

Probe. Pick a time in the past when you didn't have the fortitude to continue on with something. What learning from that set-back could fuel a new story going forward? Relate it to something that you're working on or want at the office but still haven't gotten. Can you think counterintuitively and invert one of your normal behaviors to see what happens when you act or react differently?

Probe. Think about your last performance review. What did your boss get right and get wrong in your view? How can you flip any negative perception by the next review? Make a list of the steps you can take to turn the situation around using the techniques and methods from this lesson as a guide.

Map. Make a circle divided into thirds and think about the top three priorities for your career. You can make a list of everything important to you, and then narrow it down to the top three aspects. Title? Salary? Meaning? Whatever they are, write each word in one of the three parts, then flesh it out with a description of what you want as if it has already happened and you're looking back. Ask yourself: *What do I need to do now to change my story so I ultimately get there?*

Imagine. Building on your *What's My Company's Story?* answers, can you think about one unconventional, non-traditional, unexpected thing that your company has done? What was the learning? Did the result change your company's story in some way? Looking ahead, ask: *Where can we do the unexpected and leap? What do the trends show about new opportunity areas that build on our expertise?* Doing this now will help you to share your insights later.

Authorize It! Live

Lesson Four

"I always thought that I wanted to be a creative director at an advertising agency, but now that I am one, I hate it. When I was climbing the ranks, I was prouder of my work, and realize now that part of liking it more in the past was that I didn't have to deal with all the client demands and company pressures. Now that I'm in charge, I feel sapped, like I don't have a creative bone in my body. By the time I'm done with meeting everyone else's needs and catering to what they want, there's nothing left. Also, it seems as if the whole nature of creative work is changing. Everyone operates from a place of tracking consumer behavior and then just giving more of what they click on most. Something needs to change, but I feel lost and embarrassed. I worked so hard to get here and now I don't want it."
Sarah

Sarah, the gap between expectations and reality can be a cavernous one, and the resulting disappointment that sets in is often deep and, for the most part, unproductive. It almost sounds as if you feel you have failed, or at the very least had a major lapse in judgment. But, I'm here to tell you that's not the case. Frustrations are temporary, and instead of your present situation being a predicament, it is first and foremost a win. Your Narrative and Character Arcs have brought you here, and you have snatched a brass ring on the career merry-go-round. If I viewed your H as an explorer on an odyssey, I would shout "Congratulations! You've discovered the new territory you set out to find, and you now can move on if you choose to." All that is happening is that the cycle that has led you to where you are is now complete, and it's time to begin a new quest, one that either brings the love back to the work that you're doing or leverages all that you've achieved to help you land in a better place. You don't have to settle for the status quo, you can reshape it through an unconventional lens. Here's how:

Take the lead at work. As a creative director, you have an advantage in that anything you express will resonate or at least be listened to—so ponder how you can tell a new story about the ironic lack of creativity in creative work. First, gather facts on how everything has become more transactional rather than brand-building, and the overarching implications. Identify the best examples of award-winning creative that you love and try to apply similar thinking to some of your own department's recent creative output. Then gather more information about the responsiveness to, and effectiveness of, the creative approaches you most admire. Keep anything that you say to others tightly focused on what a shift in approach would mean to the agency—this is all about making the company shine, not you.

Test. For the work you deliver to every client, you could begin inserting a bonus option that represents how you envision a possible new look and feel. Since you are moving away from the transactional clicks that they're used to, make sure to also show how this new brand-building campaign can still drive a purchasing component. Maybe your ideas—even though they weren't asked for—will slowly begin to make their way into the mix.

Also, why not ask management if you can take on a pro-bono client? Helping a cause you believe in might not only get your creative juices flowing, but it could also earn the agency some needed recognition.

Feedback. Talk to other department heads at your agency and get their hacks for handling all the administrative work involved with being a director. Since you're a creative, you might not be as versed in logistical output, so maybe their words of wisdom can help ease your administrative tasks.

Explore. Devote time each day to LinkedIn, networking, and finding companies you might like to work for, even in counterintuitive industries where you could apply your creative talents differently. You are probably just

110

one or two degrees away from anyone you might want to talk to, so begin outreach to have exploratory conversations.

Storyboard. As a fun (and revealing) game, use Infographics to tell the story of your career path, from a baby with chubby crayons and finger paints, all the way to your creative self now. Then, be fantastical and envision a bang-up ending—where could you go from here? Use all of this lesson's writerly techniques to edit your storyboard—build the anticipation for the heights you will achieve, borrow brilliance, and use surprise to delight an imagined audience with your future career exploits. Who knows? Your new resume might not be just a tried-and-true recounting of where you've been, but an entertaining vision of where you're going.

Follow up with Sharon from Lesson One:

Sharon, as you continue to move along on your quest, it's time to use the unconventional to your advantage. Here are some suggestions:

Question. You say that you're not sure how driven you are, so now is the time to get to the heart of the issue. Do you really lack drive? Or is this perception just a result of how you compare yourself to others? We all have to find our own levels of activity and balance, so to figure out what's right for you, bypass the pressure to produce and permit yourself to discover. Continue seeking the unusual in your daily life to open-up your perspective, think counterintuitively, and shift your traditional responses—the newness that bursts forth will lead you to ultimately discover your path. Ask yourself questions all along the way—be in conversation with yourself—and always drill deeper with a simple *Tell me more about*…follow-up in response to any answer that comes to mind.

Borrow Brilliance. Begin asking friends who seem to be succeeding what it's like. How did they find their passion or did it find them? Is it what they first envisioned or did it morph along the way? Be interested and learn all you can, don't be embarrassed to ask for advice, and definitely do not assume that everyone else knows some big secret. Is there something about their stories that you can apply to yours?

Revise. Your goal right now is to be an extraordinary-thinker generating a swath of options rather than deciding between two mutually-exclusive choices for your future. You're in a seek-test-learn-revise mode so there's no wrong move and nothing is written in stone. Say you discover an unexpected new passion along the way that turns into a hobby, like jewelry-making, and you decide to create custom lockets and open a shop on Etsy. If it totally and absolutely flopped, how could you weave that experience into your developing story counterintuitively? How could you own that you tried, and it didn't work out the way you expected it to? How could that experience possibly lead you to an amazing something else, whatever that may be? Shifting your perspective toward unconventional thinking will give you the creative energy to act and iterate so you can be an active participant in your future.

Lesson Five: Step Into the Unknown

A t this point, you're thinking like an author and ready to start moving your career story forward. You've established your quest, you understand the characters around you, that conflict has a purpose, and how an unconventional mindset can propel you to new levels. So now what? How do you begin to do what you need to do without feeling overwhelmed? Where should you start? If your quest still feels too enormous and impossible, just do this ONE THING: take a single step into the unknown.

What role does the unknown play in storytelling? Well, it affects almost everything! As we've seen, no story can happen without the protagonist, and perhaps the author as well, venturing into uncharted territory. Whether the main character is the underestimated H in *Legally Blonde* striking out for law school, or the tormented H in *Fleabag* who surrenders to forbidden love, fresh terrain and unexpected choices are what propel Narrative and Character Arcs forward. To solve any quest, the H must necessarily leave what they know behind. Not always entirely, but they must spurn familiar terrain at least in part to move forward and discover what's next.

So, whether you choose to tiptoe, skip or stride into the foggy unknown, you must do so because that's where the new resides. And although it's never easy, without discovering the new and confronting its associated challenges, you will literally be stuck in the same old story.

Once you release your attachment to only what is known, you open yourself up to the universe of possibility. Still, even the mightiest protagonists can display an initial hesitation, or what our story structure expert Joseph Campbell describes as a "refusal of the call." *Who me? Why me?*

Absolutely not! But eventually, all H's pick up one foot and then the other, and begin moving ahead, even though they cannot yet see what is coming. *Frozen II*'s sisters Elsa and Anna venture boldly into the unknown of enchanted forests and dark seas, and its showstopper ballad, *Into the Unknown*, underscores that it is imperative to do so, and that "Fear can't be trusted." So too must you find your own way to overcome fear and second-guessing so that you can venture beyond where you are now. Entrepreneur, entertainment world executive, and *Self Made* author Nely Galán says, "I'm afraid every day of my life. When I'm afraid, I know it's guiding me to what I must do."

So in this final lesson, you must pry yourself free from the grip of fear by doing what I advise my clients: *Go by just letting go.* With your H mindset and all that you have learned so far under your belt, it's time to release whatever has kept you from changing directions or making progress on your quest. And then ... take a considered leap. When you do, you'll find that almost immediately a string of new occurrences and realizations begin to happen that will reveal aspects and possibilities that you hadn't ever considered before. How? Because that is exactly what brand new territories do—they bring discovery and insights that will launch even more experimentation. But they also bring one more important thing—risk—which is something that most of us try to avoid at all costs.

Anytime you *Step Into the Unknown*, risk is unavoidable. That sounds daunting, I know, but here's what you need to understand: How you feel about risk is directly tied to how much you fear failure. But failure—just like obstacles or conflict—is the only way to learn the lessons you need to learn; the only way to become better, smarter, and stronger. In short, it's the only way to grow. Risk means you are trying, and never failing means you are not. If you're not failing at least occasionally, you're not making progress on your Narrative and Character Arcs. This is true in your personal life as well as your professional one. Thomas Edison said, "I didn't fail ten thousand times; I succeeded in learning that the first ten thousand didn't work until I found the one that did." Similarly, Winston Churchill said, "Success is walking from failure to failure with no loss of enthusiasm." Failure is only a waste of time if you don't learn from it. So, make it your friend at the office—fail fast, fail well, and fail forward.

When I answered a follow-up question at a recent book event, I admitted that I tend to literally trip and fall hard with some frequency. There have been four or five doozies in the last decade—ice on the sidewalk got me twice, once splitting my lip and the second time slashing my eyebrow. I once took a fall UP the stairs that broke my nose, and another time I tumbled over someone's roller-bag and broke my knee. My friends and family like to tease me about this—they find it funny that a woman who helped media empires and who earned a prime seat at the boardroom table can be completely undone by a slippery street.

But when I looked back at all of these incidents, I realized that they had one thing in common: in every instance, I fell *forward*. Not backward, not sideways, but somehow always forward. And it occurred to me that falling forward equates to something even larger; something critically important to any success I've had—I fail forward too.

Throughout my career, I never side-stepped the possibility that I might fail at work, that some grand vision of mine might not come to fruition, or that I might be dubbed foolish or inept. Instead, I took chances, I learned, I iterated, I pivoted. When I jumped in, I was all in. Many ventures in my corporate and consulting days ultimately didn't work—the new magazine that didn't find its audience, the new video technology that didn't catch fire, the breakthrough subscription model that didn't break through anything— but throughout them all, I remained in forward-mode. I'm naturally wired, it seems, to get further than I did the day before. And when failure pops up as a part of my storyline, I don't run from it, I own it.

Author, journalist, and podcaster Elizabeth Day says that her book, *How to Fail: Everything I've Ever Learned From Things Going Wrong*, is a celebration of what hasn't gone right. According to her, "Learning from our mistakes and understanding that why we fail ultimately makes us stronger … learning how to fail in life actually means learning how to succeed better."

If this doesn't describe your current worldview, reframing is in order once again. Because—trust me on this—the unknown and all of its mysterious and exciting secrets await just hoping that you'll come along. The new lives in the white space or the void between the things you already know; in the story gap that opens between wanting something and getting it. And take heart—as frightening as the unknown may appear, it inevitably contains one amazing wild card. When you do step in, *serendipity* always follows to help you on your journey, and it is as marvelous and melodious as it sounds.

Inviting Serendipity

I've always believed the adage: "When one door closes, another opens." When I left magazines behind and then chose to stop consulting to write my memoir, I stepped onto an invisible bridge to something entirely new. When I gave up my clients, I questioned my sanity, doubted my talent, stressed over lost opportunities and sacrificed income, all while sorely missing the excitement, intrigue, and camaraderie of corporate life. And then something happened. The words flowed, and I realized that I was unexpectedly writing the story that I had been born to tell.

Surrendering to an idea or a dream, or just taking chances, is the trigger for serendipity—a powerful force that almost magically opens new doors, connects the different dots that have come before, and transforms them into new shapes. Serendipity is defined as the occurrence and development of events by chance in a happy or beneficial way. But to me, the magic really kicks in when you are serendipity's *collaborator*, when you're all in and taking your own intentional actions every day. It's a working partnership—a joint venture in a way—where both you and serendipity have skin in the game. Soon you'll start to notice things clicking into place around you and you'll know that you have harnessed the energy of serendipity—and that its power is on your side.

After willingly giving up everything to write *Saturday's Child*, I knew that I still had to figure out how to rebuild my career going forward. But there was one major problem. Breaking out of my media management box to write the book had so completely transformed me, I felt that I couldn't go back to the consulting work I had done before. That said, I wasn't sure what to do next. And then, a solution serendipitously appeared.

Through a client of mine, I once had the opportunity to work with HSN and their visionary leader, Mindy Grossman, who several years later joined Weight Watchers as CEO with a mission to transform the company. Almost immediately, she instituted a new purpose, rebranded and refocused the global brand to WW, broadening its mission beyond the scale to reflect its approach to health and well-being. As I saw this work happening from afar, I wondered if there might be an opportunity for us to work together again, but I also realized that I was a small consideration given all that she intended to accomplish around the world.

I went about my life, and then one morning—serendipitously—an email "ping." Mindy had just landed from a business trip and finished *Saturday's Child* on the plane. She wrote that she found the story fascinating, and then, unexpectedly, invited me to speak at what is called "WW Inspire," an internal WW employee program to promote personal and professional development. To her, there was something unique and worth sharing about how my business mind and creative mind had fused.

As part of the prep for our interview-style discussion, I was asked what I'd like to focus on. I wondered how best to summarize my journey in a way that would have the most impact on the WW employee audience. And then it hit me—the foundation could be the *Thrive Global* article that I had just published about the five leadership lessons I learned through writing a book.

Ironically, when I was writing that piece, I had wanted to give up. I had struggled to come up with the content because the assignment was to write about leadership, and it didn't seem like there was anything new that I could add to the existing body of leadership knowledge—a simple Google search turned up more than two million results! Even though I had years of corporate experience, what would make my leadership thoughts original enough to add value and truly help someone else? I had decided to sleep on the dilemma and told myself that if something fresh didn't come to me, I would bow out.

Suddenly, the next day, the answer came. Of course! Despite having been a chief innovation officer, the writing was the key. My immersion in the world of storytelling had made me see lessons and leadership truths I had never recognized before writing a book. The process had given me a way to crystallize and articulate what I had learned in business over the years in a way that was new and palatable for anyone at any stage of their career. I quickly jotted down the five lessons for success and gave them each a writing-themed title. When it was published, the *Thrive Global* interview was shared online and, a few months later, when I shared the concept with the team at WW, they loved it.

The presentation day finally came. The session was live-streamed to WW employees around the world, and even though it was a bit nerve-wracking, I was surprised to discover just how much I enjoyed sharing how to *author-ize* your life. Even though I had never envisioned myself inspiring employees before, I felt that I had somehow stumbled into my perfect zone—a marriage of the personal and professional, of strategy and creativity, of advice and perspective that could help others. And best of all, the talk seemed to be a hit.

Afterward, I realized that what I had put together for WW was replicable and that I could secure the same type of opportunity at many other companies. That thought—solution, really—was a saving grace. It hit just at the right time as I was wondering what to do next.

More talks at top companies followed, and then along came the opportunity to develop it into an online course. In the process of outlining the course, I realized that I had also outlined my next book. In a career of long hours and hard work, writing *Saturday's Child* had been the hardest work I'd ever done. In fact, whenever people asked me what book I was writing next, I always answered: *I haven't recovered from this one.* Yet suddenly I seemed to be ready to do it again. The truth was that I knew I could only write a second book if I found a topic that had as much *real meaning* for others. Now, serendipitously, I did—and *Authorize It!* was born. Throughout it all, the unknown had held the answers that I was seeking and revealed them to me over time.

Who knows what the unknown holds next for me or for any of us? That's what makes the mystery of it so exciting.

At Your Desk

How can we best leverage the unknown to win at work? And how do we minimize floundering and maximize flourishing when we can't actually see what's ahead? Here are four tactics that can help you march into the unknown with grace so that it can lead you where you need to go.

Tactic #1: ASSUREDNESS

Ever hear of writer's block? People at work often have this same lack of confidence, and the antidote—for writers and for the H that is you—is to have the courage to still take action despite misgivings and unease. Trust in yourself and trust the master Narrative Arc—the flow is leading you somewhere, things will sort out, and the dots of your life will ultimately connect to form your future. You can be certain of this, even in the midst of uncertainty, and when you surrender to this notion you will find that it bestows the confidence we all need.

H's can be afraid, but they cannot operate from a place of fear. The business world can be a judgmental one, full of sniping, competition, and comparison that makes us feel inferior. Your talent and output are watched and critiqued every step of the way. But as SuperSoulSunday speaker and author Mastin Kipp writes in his book, *Claim Your Power:* "When you are afraid to take action because there is an outcome you fear, not taking the action produces the outcome you're afraid of." For example, maybe you tend to fly under the radar at work—you don't speak up in meetings, you don't volunteer, and you don't ask for what you need. Why? Because you fear that if you're visible, people will find out that you might not know what you're doing, and you'll get fired. Well, in the next round of lay-offs, you may become the first one to go because no one is too sure about how important you are to the mix. The fear of getting fired—in this case, your intentional invisibility—might be what ultimately gets you fired. So you need to brace yourself for the criticism that is the inevitable result of putting yourself out there—and put yourself out there anyway.

Once, I spearheaded the pilot for a new entertainment magazine that I believed had a real shot for success. The timing was right, the audience was hungry for the content, and the advertisers seemed willing to support it. I dove in with enthusiasm, but it soon became clear that management's actual investment was much lower than planned. Progress naturally slowed, but the lack of forward-motion was criticized and perceived as my fault rather than a result of their own financial reality. Another time when I was consulting, a digital client brought me on to oversee brand strategy but then switched to focus on a heavily regulated industry where I was not an expert. Suddenly, I went from irreplaceable to very expendable.

These two painful examples—pulled from many such moments over an entire career—show you that I've been there and understand just how it feels when confidence and pride take a hit. When you're embarrassed and infuriated at the same time; when you're kicking yourself for making the wrong choice; when you feel others are unfairly discrediting you. In these dark moments, the unknown gives you only one option to reclaim your assuredness: be grateful for the learning the situation brings and how it allows you to fail forward and emerge stronger.

I remain grateful for how valuable both of those steps into the unknown were to me. Many of the relationships I built from those two projects came back around to enhance my life later on—the magazine client introduced me to interesting connections in the entertainment world and taught me to always tie deliverables to specific investment levels; the digital client introduced me to one person who led me to another, who then opened the door to this book. Along with recognizing my "mistakes" like not getting enough confirmation of important aspects upfront, seeing the good that ultimately came from both incidents renews my confidence and mitigates any fear of missteps.

These days criticism might not come from your boss or your colleagues—it can emanate from all those opinionated strangers on social media who can say anything they want, and then spread it around. In these situations, you quickly learn that you can't please everyone and that there is always someone who will actively dislike you and/or your work—and relish saying so. Writers are no strangers to this phenomenon—when they put themselves and their work out into the world, literary reviews and reader reactions always follow. Even though author Delia Owens's *Where the Crawdads Sing* has been hailed as a masterpiece, six percent of its thirty-four thousand reviews on Amazon are three stars or less, which means more than two thousand disappointed readers. Once again, criticism from some corner is inevitable when you are taking risks. If its sting is high on your list of fears that keep you from moving forward, it's time to reframe.

Fear Not!

These writerly insights should provide some comfort:

Fear strikes everyone—even the most confident person sitting at your conference table is afraid—and continually struggling with some amount of fear is perfectly normal.

Fear can heighten our senses and make us feel acutely aware and alive, which can help us reframe it—think of your fears as exciting rather than terrifying.

Total fearlessness is unattainable—and unwise—because there are times when you *should* be afraid. This isn't about being fearless—it's about not letting fear stand in the way of you taking considered actions or making calculated decisions that could benefit you.

When you actively deal with fear, it makes you vulnerable. Nobody likes to be vulnerable, but as we saw in Lesson Two, it's actually a good thing. In *Saturday's Child*, I revealed a limiting belief instilled by my unconventional upbringing that I had kept hidden for years in order to not appear weak. Although I imagined all sorts of horrors when the book was released, I got a counterintuitive surprise. Guess what I hear about from readers all the time? How strong and brave I am. Vulnerability is powerful and you are always in control of what you choose to reveal.

Tactic #2: ASPIRATION

As an ambitious H, you should always surround yourself with the best and brightest minds. People smarter than you should not intimidate, rather they should inspire you to greater heights and give you the confidence to step into the unknown.

As part of your active aspiration, seek help and advice from people you admire as you figure out your first steps into uncharted territory. Every writer knows just how crucial feedback is to the process of creating a great story, especially when you are unsure of which way to go next. Authors cannot exist in the vacuum of only their own thoughts, and at some point, other smart voices must enter the mix. Everyone can learn something and benefit from other people and their feedback, especially in the unknown.

If you feel that you've gotten to a point where you just can't go further on your own, seeking *constructive* criticism from others who you respect can help you define your next steps, just like an author whose editor provides manuscript guidance or whose early readers share their thoughts. To best navigate and innovate in unknown territory, be sure to collaborate, listen, and tweak until all the parts combine into a clearer whole.

Continue to bring an adventurous, enterprising, forward-looking attitude to work that announces just how curious, open, and positive you are—a team player who is always willing to try, a seeker who will tirelessly strive to uncover the best solution even when there are far more questions than answers. These traits will soon have others aspiring to be like you. And through it all, make daydreaming about what you want to happen a regular part of your inner life. Visualize scenes, fantasize about conversations you could have, and always act "as if" what you want can actually happen—and then let those images populate the pages of your mind.

Tactic #3: ACTUALIZATION

The unknown—the blank canvas, the empty space of possibility—is vital to your journey of becoming. Your self-actualization, or character journey, is one part, but improving your story at work is also about the actualization of ideas. In *The Creativity Leap: Unleash Curiosity, Improvisation, and Intuition at Work*, creativity strategist and author Natalie Nixon defines creativity as "our ability to toggle between wonder and rigor to solve problems and produce novel value."

Idea actualization really all comes down to the *rigorous action* that is a necessary component of every story. Actively bringing every ounce of your tenacity, precision, and determination to whatever it is you have conceived is what separates the doers from the dreamers. But implementing anything might seem completely out-of-reach when you are taking your first steps into the unknown.

Persevering in the face of uncertainty is something that writers understand deep within their hearts. A blank page is the ultimate "unknown." Because authors are used to staring at them, they quickly learn to spontaneously actualize—even if they aren't entirely sure where they are going—because if they don't write, nothing happens. Writing is a process of discovery within the zone of the personal unknown. If you ask any author why they write, the most common answer is to make sense of things. How? Because as you write, thoughts get sorted and worked out on the page. New creative discoveries, ideas, and solutions hit most often when we're smack in the middle of doing something and not simply thinking about it. Most of the time, what writers have in their heads at the beginning is different from the finished product—even a screenwriter's final script that has already been edited a hundred times changes anew when the actors begin to speak the words.

For you, all this translates to one actualization fact: you'll never know how to solve a problem or find your way through a situation until you dive in. Maybe you have an inkling of something, but until you actually start playing around with it—talking about it, trying to use language to articulate it—you don't really know what could be possible. So follow a writer's lead, be proactive, and take responsibility because everything comes from you. The beginning of any project, any goal, any quest, is in your hands. Unless you give yourself the green light and *Step Into the Unknown* by putting that first word on the metaphorical page, nothing will happen. Even if you don't feel fully ready, the quest must begin. You can't overthink it—just set the intention and act.

In unknown territory, begin to actualize with small steps before all the answers are known to learn along the way. Your creative problem-solving will naturally become a two-step process that combines extraordinary-think brainstorming of new possibilities with subsequent ordinary-think as you evaluate the best of the bunch. Then you'll begin to form a concrete roadmap or plan with defined milestones and goals. And all along the way, be sure to have a *Yes, and* mindset rather than a *No, but* mentality. Those two little words—Yes, and—can unleash superpowers and build upon anything.

Tactic #4: ARTISTIC EXCELLENCE

Mercedes Benz's one-time slogan, *The Pursuit of Excellence,* underscores the brand's unceasing commitment to quality, high standards, performance, and artful design. It conveys that they are never satisfied and always in a race with themselves to live up to their potential.

Although there are subtle differences between artistry and excellence, they are inextricably linked. Both help you to live up to your potential and get you to your personal best every time. Excellence—being outstanding or exceptional—is easy to connect to success. If you pursue excellence with every endeavor, you will ultimately achieve. But many people struggle with the concept of artistry—doing something creative with a flair that makes it dazzling, moving, and compelling—so they decide to narrowly define themselves as either artistic or not (and most often as not).

But I guarantee you that *you are* artistic because, by nature, all of us are curious, creative beings. Being artistic at work simply means being thoughtful when approaching or solving something—it's *how* you do what you do.

Writers live up to their potential by pursuing artistic excellence at every juncture. They continually dip into the well of their innate creativity and strive to achieve their personal best with each scene they write. For you to best navigate the dissonance of the unknown, you must develop the artistic creativity that lives within you while you also pursue excellence in everything you do.

Artistry

To harness the potential of the artistic excellence within you, try these tactics:

Plug into a passion to get your creative juices flowing. The passion may have nothing to do with your work life, and sometimes it's better if it doesn't. Because artistry is like a bridge between your conscious and unconscious mind, doing something—anything—that is creative will get those ideas flowing and help you take your thinking and output to the next level.

Make space for creativity to emerge by embracing an "incompleteness" mindset vs. a completist one—there's peace in the notion that everything around us is constantly changing and evolving and some new facet or perspective will always appear.

Rethink how *not knowing* is really an asset. How could that be? Well, not being bound by preconceived notions can be liberating because you are free to discover what is off the beaten path—the vast unseen—and present ideas or solutions that break new ground.

Ruminate to hear your inner artistic voice. Even though thunderbolts of ideas and solutions can strike in the midst of action and doing, every writer also knows that solitude and quiet are required at some point every day. So also seek times where you can eliminate all the noise and distractions that can drown out ideas or daydreams trying to bubble to the surface. Press pause to stoke your creative fires by taking a walk, meditating, or exercising ... and watch what happens.

Overcoming Doubt

Fear and doubt are closely related but are full of subtle differences. Fear is instinctual preservation; it is your adrenaline-fueled alarm bell that rings in response to an actual or perceived threat. Doubt, on the other hand, is disbelief that calls into question the truth of something, and this uncertainty is shaped more by your own life experiences.

Like fear, doubt strikes everyone: H's who question the value of their mission, sensitive writers (a.k.a. all writers) who think their work won't measure up, or executives who worry that sooner or later everyone will find out that they're imposters. As you begin to venture into the unknown, you will likely doubt yourself at almost every turn. Especially when you don't know exactly where you're going, it's easy to have misgivings about absolutely everything.

Whether you're making a broader life change or focused on a specific project at the office, second-guessing your choices, decisions, and actual talent (or lack thereof) is par for the course when you are in a state of ambiguity. In fact, normal doubts are magnified after your project gets underway. Why? Because the messy middle—the space or the story gap between the beginning and the outcome—is where all the really hard work is.

Every writer knows this from experience. Beginnings and endings are always easier and more exciting to write than those long, sometimes cloudy, plodding middles. The middle is where the story has the greatest risk of lagging, where momentum slows, and even an H with a promising start can meander into boring or tedious territory. There have been volumes written with instructions for writers on how to forge on and avoid getting stuck in a mess—and this wisdom can help you too.

At work, after the heady rush of beginning something new, doubt and reluctance can appear. Suddenly, you become aware of all the challenging work that lies ahead, of how there are no easy answers, and how every step forward seems to kick off an unintended consequence or a new problem. You know that the story should be picking up steam but feel added pressure when you realize that it's not. You're faced with "scope creep" that turns five deliverables into ten, or the difficulty of running a cross-functional project in a siloed company, or the uncooperativeness of disgruntled team members. It's easy to become convinced that you're not suited for the project, that you never should have undertaken it, and that salvaging anything may be impossible. Writers must sometimes confront the reality that a story needs major revisions or even starting from scratch. Similarly, some part or even all of what you have done so far might need to be scrapped. More likely, however, the forces that are causing your doubts are just one of the inevitable challenges on your quest or in your Character Arc—you are simply facing a mountain that you will eventually find a way to climb. Rest assured that you may not need to crumple up the paper and start over because you can find your way around most obstacles with an edit or a pivot.

Here are some story strategies for the moments when you feel like giving in to doubts and insecurities, or just need to fire-up your faltering middle:

Strategy #1: INTRODUCE

The easiest way to fix a flagging middle is to bring something new into the equation, the way a writer may insert a new character or plot twist at this point to shake things up. At work, you too should consider inserting something fresh into the process to keep yourself and others moving forward. Perhaps an additional team member with a missing skill set can be added or brought into one meeting as a guest. Or maybe you can bypass a roadblock by changing lanes to work on a different aspect of the project. Or you can try to incite action with a spontaneous brainstorm, a fun incentive, or an anonymous survey of team members to collect insights that they may be unwilling to say aloud. You could even accelerate the timeline to light a fire under everyone (yes, that is more pressure, but it's also how diamonds are made) or conversely, slow down by building a completely unrelated creative conversation into your next session. The point is, using your imagination when energy and enthusiasm are dropping can inject new life into your work story.

Sometimes a middle gets messy because you realize that you need to know more about the area you're working in or what you're trying to solve. You can gather that information by crafting a market overview akin to a detailed backstory for a fictional world, or by creating an ideal customer persona, just like a character profile. Give that persona a name, create a-day-in-her-life populated with all she does from the moment she wakes up until she turns out the light. Such an exercise may lead you to see a new opportunity for action and new plot points.

Also, keep in mind that some of the best plot twists happen when the writer *purposely misdirects* the reader to think one way about a person or an event, and then surprises them with a whole different truth or reality. This may be happening in your messy middle. Since we can never know everything, ask yourself if something has been missed, if you've been misdirected, or if you're operating on assumptions that could be false. If you think this might be the case, introduce a new piece of information through a social media poll or informal focus group to see murky aspects of your project more clearly. The goal is always to improve the ending by clarifying and pumping up the middle.

Strategy #2: ISOLATE

Sometimes it is best to identify the result or outcome you would like and then detach from it. The best endings come when the middles are equally fascinating and fruitful, so after you isolate the outcome you would like, don't be afraid to take your eye off the finish and make the most of the process along the way.

Of course, it's important to be clear about what you want to happen—vague end goals can sink a project before it starts—but you should always keep your options open to what *might* happen. There's power in detachment because holding on too tightly can impede progress—if we're too attached to the results we want, we can miss an important discovery along the way. If you find it hard to let go of pulling all the strings, just have faith in the Narrative Arc's cycles which demonstrate over and over that it all will work out with some transformation in the end.

Stay present in the moment, break down the problems at hand, and then —as a writer would—consider if you need to break apart the middle so you actually have two endings, one smaller and one bigger finale. For example, the MVP (minimum viable product) mentality can create a "soft" launch to gather feedback from a group of early adopters that can then be applied to whatever you have in the works.

Once, a client of mine created a team dedicated to expanding a profitable weekend craft marketplace. We went into the project assuming that the solution would be to simply add more locations throughout the country, so we set out to find the best new spots. But the more research we did, the more we discovered that such an expansion would put enormous pressure on our most important vendors. It was also way more difficult than we'd expected to find new fairgrounds in places that matched our purchasing demographic. All seemed lost in the messy middle of that project, with absolutely nothing to show after weeks of effort.

At that point, we introduced a group we hadn't talked to before—consumers who had previously attended the markets—and asked them some questions.

Predictably, the concept of more locations was meaningless to them, because our present audience saw no reason to travel to a new location if they had one nearby. But they did have a suggestion that was quite meaningful: Why not create an online marketplace so they could shop year-round instead of at just one event? That feedback set a completely unexpected new venture into motion. The best solution may be entirely different from what you or your boss imagine—in fact, the messy middle may hold a bigger, better problem for you to solve.

Strategy #3: *INNOVATE*

When facing the natural potholes and uncertainty of the middle, it's time to recharge and re-envision. By definition, innovation implies an arrival in unknown territory, so the first thing you need to do to conceive something new is to step into the empty space. Then, to harness your innovative mindset—the one that is laser-focused on actively creating rather than on just reacting—identify the new problems in front of you. When you do, refer back to your Character Arc with a little self-inquiry to see if you are contributing to the stalling in some way: *Am I getting caught up in unnecessary drama? Is something holding me back? Is there inner discord in my way?* And always push yourself to rise above by asking, *Can I do more or do it differently?*

Then let your extraordinary-think imagination run wild. Create a writer's storyboard to visualize the problems as "scenes," and continue asking: *What plot twists can fix this and how can I make them happen?* Shake up your workplace and any daily routine: if you meet in the morning, switch to the afternoon; if you usually start your team meeting with a recap, open instead with a vision of what you want to accomplish; if you typically end with a to-do list, switch to a discussion about each person's favorite company and why they made the cut.

As a chief innovation officer, I was part-entrepreneur (charged with developing new businesses and business models), and part-intrapreneur (responsible for helping to transform the company for the digital future ahead). The role of the unknown in entrepreneurship is easily explained—you are supposed to explore, create, and birth the new. But *intra*preneurship is more amorphous, mysterious, and treacherous. Why? Because it's an "inside job," and deep inner work is required to transform something that already exists into something else. Projects that are designed to reimagine the inner workings of a company and improve a future bottom line often have the messiest middles of all, and intrapreneurship is usually met with resistance to change every step of the way.

I had to execute on both intrapreneurship and entrepreneurship every day in my role as CIO, and when my publishing company was acquired by a more powerful media entity, I was at it again. I joined that new company's executive ranks as an innovation consultant to help them navigate unknown territories and spot unseen opportunities. At the outset, their magazine division knew they did not have all the answers, but they were certain of one thing—if they were going to thrive, there needed to be a total mindset-shift about how they created and delivered content in a changing world.

I had a lead role on a high-level team that worked in tandem with both the President and COO. The company's story needed to change and the Narrative Arc for that evolution was as intricate and complex as an arc can be, full of simultaneous mini-arcs and subplots. To begin, we identified the company's overarching quest—*to transform from month to moment*—and we set out to overhaul content, products, and services from the monthly schedule of magazines to every minute of every day.

The entrepreneurial part was all fun and games, full of identifying our assets, researching consumer behavior, building customer personas, and tracking trends as well as the big calendar moments where millions of women moved in unison. We soon buzzed with a hundred product ideas to deliver our content in new ways—from fitness boot camps to career jumpstarts; holiday parties-in-a-box to new-year-new-you diet tools; fashion apps to gift registries; dating survival guides to online education—and identified many new partnerships and potential acquisitions that would help manifest our new reality.

But oh, that intrapreneurship part wasn't fun at all. In order to transform from month to moment, the way that the entire, giant company operated had to change. New skill sets were needed, which meant hirings and firings; new structures were necessary, which meant different hierarchies and cross-platform departments and divisions; new objectives and incentives were required, which meant revising goals and employee rewards. In other words, *everything* had to shift if we were going to steer this Titanic safely to a new shore. It was a hard slog through unknown seas with a very deep and turbulent middle. But what allowed me to help them innovate and win, I realize now, was that all along the way, I was thinking like a writer who was composing a new story.

Now, you too will be a step ahead in the innovation game, able to play beautifully in both arenas. You'll excel with intrapreneurship because its challenges are akin to the inner work that every H is faced with on their journeys—and maintaining an intrapreneurial mindset at the office will be easier because you've been doing the inner work on yourself. And you'll thrive at entrepreneurship now that *Authorize It!* has sparked your expansive extraordinary-think inventiveness at every point between ideation and implementation. Your ability to find opportunities in the unknown will boost your employability and propel your success.

What's Next?

You have now crossed a threshold of awareness and are forever changed. You won't see things the same way, believe the same things, or make the same decisions. Now that you know, there's no turning back—the power to shape your story and the story of your career is in your hands. Radio personality and author Ira Glass says, "Great stories happen to people who can tell them." True, but I would rephrase the sentiment: "Great stories happen to people who think like the writers who tell them."

What great story will you tell and how will you tell it? The next chapter— *Authorize It!: Tell Your Stories*—will pull all that you've learned from these five lessons together so you can do just that. Now, your only path is forward and your only way is up.

Prompts

Ponder. This final *What's My Story?* installment is designed to keep the future of your story unfolding as powerfully as possible. From your incident that took you through the four cycles, ask yourself: *What did I learn about my ability to thrive in unknown territory? Are there positive responses and approaches that I can incorporate into my story going forward?* Then, recall a time when something unexpected happened. What you were doing before it happened? List the sequence of events and serendipitous occurrences that preceded it and pinpoint *your role* in generating those dot-connecting moments. Ask: *How can I stay open to possibility so the unexpected continues to enhance my story?*

Probe. Pick one person each day and ask: *What is the most interesting new thing you're working on or doing?* Observe how they describe a new passion, project, or discovery, and then ask one of these follow-ups: *What led you to it? How did it change along the way?*

Probe. Are you better at extraordinary-thinking (brainstorming new possibilities) or ordinary-thinking (deciding between two possibilities)? Can you think of ways to better balance both actions so you can be even more effective? Can you think of a time where your final choice between two things evolved into a middle-ground alternative between them?

Create. Start a business book club at the office that meets monthly over lunch. Choose a book like Robert Iger's *The Ride of a Lifetime: Lessons Learned From 15 Years as CEO of the Walt Disney Company*, and meet to discuss it as a group. Not only will it be enlightening for all participants, but it will allow everyone to step into new territory together.

Identify. Pick one new thing to do each day for a week. Nothing grand, it can be as small as testing a new tea or cold-brew coffee. Just be sure to sprinkle a little newness into every twenty-four hours and watch it build from there. Including a meditation, exercise, or spiritual practice will further help you get comfortable with the unknown and stay in the present, rather than in the future.

Identify. Keep practicing your storytelling skills, especially as you navigate the unknown. Identify possible storylines for any thorny issue or idea using a fill-in-the-blank story template. This concept works just as well now as it did in elementary school:

- **"Once Upon a Time"** _____(fill in the Shift that is putting you into unknown territory)

- **Then**_____(fill in an
  Instability)
- **And then**_____(add more
  Instability)
- **But then**_____(add an
  intense Darkness moment)
- **And then**_____(add the
  evolution in the Light)

Imagine. Building on your *What's My Company's Story?* answers, know that your company's story is as impacted by risk, failure, and the unknown as is yours. Think about how your company really views all three: Do they say one thing but mean another? Does doubt ever creep in to create hesitancy when they make decisions? What would getting comfortable with the unknown enable them to do that they're not doing now? And finally, ask yourself: *What can I apply from all I've learned about the power of the unknown and being comfortable with uncertainty to my company?*

Authorize It! Live

Lesson Five

"I took a safe job years ago because my dream of being a painter seemed out of reach. In my childhood home, my creativity wasn't really seen as a way to earn a living and having something to fall back on was reinforced at every turn. It seemed at the time as if I needed benefits, a steady paycheck, and a 401K. I always thought I'd be able to somehow do both, but then I got married and had children, and that plan went out the window. Now my kids are getting older, but even though I took the safe route, I still don't have the financial ability to live my dream. And even if I did, I wouldn't know where to begin. What are my options to finally get what I want?"
Pauline

Pauline, early in life, you stepped into the *known* (or at least, the more predictable), rather than the unknown. And that's fine. Most of us have necessary vocations that take precedence over our avocations. Just like the seasons of story structure, there is a time in everyone's life when they have to do something they may not want to do, in order to do whatever they want down the road.

Today, many macro-trends point toward multiple careers in our lifetimes. Not only are we living longer, but the corporate world is shifting dramatically, as is the nature of the work we do. So, rather than doing one thing inside of a company for our entire career, we will all have to be more entrepreneurial, continually redefining what we do and how we do it all along the way. Which also means a lot more steps into the unknown than ever before.

It sounds daunting, but it's really good news for us all. It means that there's a long road ahead, so take heart; I published my first book at an age when people in prior generations were usually thinking about retirement. That said, what I hear from women everywhere is that the financial piece is what most often holds them back from living their dreams.

You've been a practical person this far, and I'm here to tell you that sensibility will still have a place as you chase your dream. Most people cannot step away from a steady income and move right into something new —there needs to be a transition period, and you might even have to invest a bit in yourself and your new endeavor in a way that will pay-off when it fully actualizes.

The eighty-twenty percent business rule for innovation works here: keep doing what you're doing but find a way to devote twenty percent of your time to that Visionary level where you begin to figure out, test, and take steps toward what's next for you. Which means that you're going to have to work harder than ever before. There's just no getting around the persistence, dedication, and rolling-up-of-sleeves that birthing something new requires. But, as they say, if you love what you're doing, it doesn't feel like work (although I guarantee that you'll be more tired). Here is some guidance to help you *Step Into the Unknown*:

Invite serendipity by actualizing your talent for painting by taking classes, sketching friends, participating in silent auctions with a piece, offering to teach a class at schools, or giving mini paintings as birthday presents. Step into your artistry, practice your creativity, and demonstrate it to the world and to those around you in some way every day.

Introduce something fresh into the work you've always done—and use it as a way to open new doors and meet new people. Work with a different medium: if you're a watercolorist, try multi-media; if you're an oil painter, try digital filters for your work. Take classes to grow these skills. The options are practically infinite, so bottom line: inject the new.

Isolate some local gallery targets and then detach from the long-term goal of a solo exhibition to see what you can gain in the meantime. Devote yourself to volunteering, even if it's just for one Saturday a month. Be sure to strike up conversations with owners, co-workers, and patrons to see if they'd be open to giving you feedback on your own work.

Innovate and be non-traditional as you think about ways to use your talent for painting to open new doors—and earn some money. Approach local home stagers and offer to create large-scale abstract work at a reasonable fee for empty walls or present yourself as a wedding scene painter who comes to the reception and completes a work of art at the event. Think differently as you venture into unknown territory.

By stepping in, doing, letting go of outcomes, and seeing what connects, you will begin to pave a new road for yourself.

Follow-up with Sharon from Lesson One:

Sharon, hopefully, you have arrived at this fifth lesson in a vastly different place from where you began. Now, here are some additional thoughts on how stepping into the unknown can help you round out all that you have absorbed thus far.

When you initially said, "Nothing seems to happen for me," it sounded as if you're in waiting mode, expecting that your passion will suddenly appear and fall into your outstretched arms. It's crucial that you begin to trade passivity for action, and this is where stepping into the unknown can help.

Begin to do and explore new things that excite your soul, even if they are unrelated to anything you've done before or to work. It's important to test new ways of being and doing so that you can learn what you don't like or want on the way to discovering what you do. Poke around other industries and job functions, visit museums or take a trip to a cultivated garden, listen to inspirational podcasts like *OnBeing*, or to author talks about any kind of book. The possibilities for expanding your horizons are endless.

And when something does click or pique your interest, know that you don't have to fling yourself headfirst into a new business or career path. Make your first attempt akin to the discovery phase of nearly every work project. Find opportunities or classes that will give you more information.

Enroll in a business course to gather knowledge if you think you do want to create your own business one day, or in a graphic arts class if you're wondering whether you might want to do something creative. New insight will appear as you seek unconventional paths in unknown territory.

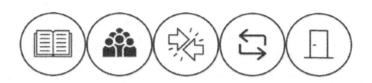

Chapter Six: Authorize It!—Tell Your Stories

Congratulations! You've made it through all five lessons, and you've worked hard to understand story structure, characters, conflict, unconventionality, and the unknown. You've mapped your own inner journey, built your Protagonist and Supporting Character Profiles, pondered compelling answers to all the *What's My Story?* Prompts, and imagined answers to the *What's My Company's Story?* Prompts.

Now, this chapter is your ***action plan—the storytelling workbook that pulls it all together***—so that you can *authorize* stories about yourself, your company, and your brands, products, or ideas to make them resonate and connect emotionally with others. From here on, you will be able to tell stories that deepen relationships with your bosses, co-workers, clients, partners, and customers. And they will be stories that get you closer to *YES* and to the results that you want.

So let's activate all your "think like a writer" skills within these three easy steps:

- STEP #1: **Crafting** your personal story.
- STEP #2: **Telling** your personal story.
- STEP #3: **Animating** your company's story.

STEP #1: Crafting Your Personal Story

As the writer, editor, producer, and director of your life—*and* as the H—you never want to hand your story or narrative over to anyone else. You define yourself, and once you do, you can fully embody it so others will think differently about you and what you're capable of. To do this, you need to come up with your **Defining Line.**

In the publishing and entertainment worlds, a line that says it all is called a keynote or a logline, and you've seen them in teasers for movies and in headlines for books on Amazon. And with their business taglines, companies do the same—from L'Oréal's "Because You're Worth It," to DeBeer's "A Diamond is Forever," a tagline is the forty-thousand-foot view of what that company is and does.

Getting to the crux of it, though, is the hardest part. Businesses pay advertising agencies large sums to come up with a line that perfectly expresses their reason for being, while authors struggle mightily with the sentence that clearly conveys the essence of their eighty-thousand-word book. If you're thinking, *How can I possibly summarize where I'm going and what I stand for in a line?* fear not—we'll follow the same process a writer uses to pinpoint their story's highest expression.

Action #1: FIND YOUR BACKSTORY

Let's begin by gathering all your answers to:

- Your five *What's My Story?* Ponder Prompts (one from each Lesson).
- Your fictionalized Protagonist Profile (from Lesson Two).
- The three Inner Journey questions (from Lesson Two, after the Supporting Character questions).

Now let's look at the whole of your answers and find the threads that connect all of these different pieces of you. Look for themes and patterns between all of your answers, and then extract what they reveal about your character:

- What did you learn about yourself—your emotions, actions, reactions, and ability to navigate conflict, uncertainty, and the unknown—from the incident that took you through the Narrative Arc cycles?

- What were the newfound strengths and positives hidden within your *What's My Story?* incident. Did it take you from pain to a power that you didn't know you had before? What can you leverage going forward?
- How does your real-life incident compare to your Protagonist Profile's fictionalized hopes, dreams, and disappointments? What are the similarities and differences? What traits can you connect and amplify going forward?

Action #2: HIGHLIGHT YOUR POSITIVES

Again, looking at the answers you've gathered, list only how you've evolved positively and the strengths that allowed you to do so. This list of personal positives—be they actual or aspirational—are the keywords that *you want to define you*, so add even more now if they come to mind. Should this tally feel incomplete, you can get an additional spark by pulling the good things that have been said about you into an *It's a Wonderful Life* file. Just like that classic story, we all need to be reminded of how our deeds impact and touch others. From compliments and thank-yous to congratulations and reviews, read through each one and note the common themes. If you still need more positives, take the ten-minute *VIA Institute on Character* survey at viacharacter.org that many businesses offer to their employees.

Action #3: SPOTLIGHT YOUR VALUES

Next, make a list of what it is that you *value* most. These values are three-fold:

- **Your core personal beliefs**—from commitment to devotion, courage to honesty, compassion to loyalty—list what you value most and what motivates and guides you.
- **Your career dreams**—your work quest—that you value and want to work towards. Do you want to design cool spaces? Develop drug

141

therapies? Create digital products? Note the career path that would add the most value to your life.

- **Your ideal audience groups, industries, or causes** that you value the most and would like to have benefit from your efforts. The environment? The under-served? Youth or the elderly? Niche target? Zoom in on who or what you'd like to serve to round out your values.

Action #4: DETERMINE YOUR WHO, WHAT, WHEN, WHERE, WHY & HOW

Next, let's build the foundation of your Defining Line with the simple five W's and one H used by journalists whenever they report a story. With your answers to the three Actions above in mind, now answer these questions:

- **Who** is the H you aspire to be?_____
- **What** is your quest?_____
- **When** does it happen?_____
- **Where** does it take place?_____
- **Why** do you want to do it and who will it benefit?_____
- **How** will you accomplish it?_____

(To complete the How, just write down all the actions you will take, including your methods, approach, and even your personal style while accomplishing it. Then distill all into a one-line answer, something like *I will take five small steps every day to get me closer to my quest*—getting up an hour earlier, approaching research, outreach, and training with determination, and acting as if I already have achieved the dream.)

The Result: YOUR DEFINING LINE

Now it's time to use the above answers as inspiration for your own Defining Line—your personal mission statement, or what corporate-speak would describe as your personal brand DNA.

When I was transitioning from media consultant to author, speaker, and coach, I used these same exercises to craft my Defining Line: *To illuminate possibility and inspire professionals to reach their career potential.*

This highest-level expression serves as a filter for my actions every single day. It helps me to define myself in conversation and to navigate potential opportunities so that I can determine where I should put my energy—if I'm considering a project that doesn't seem like it will advance this vision, I say no. Staying true to this promise led to my memoir, speaking opportunities, workshops, an online course, and to this book.

Like any art, storytelling not only requires vision and creativity, it requires practice. Have a look at some LinkedIn "tagline" descriptions of people in an industry you'd like to be in—or even Instagram bio lines of people you admire—and keep playing with your answers and practicing until you get to a line that reflects who you are and where you're going. And once you do, fully own it! Make your new character and narrative real by living and breathing and *messaging* it.

STEP #2: Telling Your Personal Story

What often trips up writers is their hesitancy to market themselves and their masterpieces. Yet they know that even if they manage to write the best book ever, people can't read it if they don't know about it. There is a vast middle ground between shy self-effacement and shameless self-promotion, and any successful writer needs to get comfortable in that white space—and so do you!

Now that you've got your story, it's time to tell it. To demonstrate your Defining Line, plant seeds for it, broadcast it, and plaster it wherever you can. Television producer and writer—and author of the bestselling book, *Year of Yes: How to Dance It Out, Stand In the Sun and Be Your Own Person*— Shonda Rhimes says: "You know what I am? I am smart, I am talented, I take advantage of the opportunities that come my way and I work really, really hard. Don't call me lucky. Call me a badass." I call her an H who is on top of her messaging and storytelling game.

You need to embrace the same marketing mindset to convey your value —and the value of the work that you are doing—through your own words and actions. How you message yourself, your responsibilities, your project results, and your suggestions for new initiatives determines how effective you will be. You want to accomplish this messaging through Description, Demonstration, and Dialogue, three tools that writers use to convey the personality, skills, and purpose of their characters.

- **Description.** Descriptive language is a writer's forte, and you need to capitalize on the catchphrases, adjectives, adverbs, and accomplishments that best describe you and who you want to be. Are you an out-of-the-box thinker? Solution finder? Team player? Once you find your words, use them! To give you an example, some words and phrases that I use about myself are ideator, creative-meets-strategist, business sage, intuitive innovator, transformative trainer, opportunity diviner, possibility coach, mentoring maverick, and so on. Once you have your own, you can work them into the appropriate office and networking conversations, your team bio, resume, and LinkedIn profile.
- **Demonstration.** You need to actively demonstrate your best tendencies and traits to make them real for others. Remember how writers show something and not just tell it? This principle applies to demonstration one thousand percent. To become truly known for a particular talent, others must see and feel it in *action*. An H can't just tell people they're a problem-solver, they have to show that they effectively solve them. So for all those descriptor words or phrases that you want to define you, show what you're made of and capable of by living them.
- **Dialogue.** Whether through emails, texts, calls, or face-to-face conversations, the direct communication and exchanges you have with others are an essential opportunity for you to tell your story, in whole or in part, to move your quest and opportunities forward. This can be baffling for some and terrifying for others, so I've created READ—a simple template that brings together all of the

144

storytelling secrets to help you *authorize* any personal and business story that you need to tell for maximum impact.

Introducing READ

READ is a story-shaping tool, a four-part sequential path that is grounded by the Narrative Arc's cycles. READ helps you to instantly connect, get to the point, and put your listener right into your story so that they can see how much better things will be with you rather than without you:

R = **Relate** to some challenge or *Shift* that's happening in the larger world— a problem or situation that you and they are experiencing.

E = **Ease** the *Instability* from the situation that is swirling around you both with an idea or solution that you want them to accept.

A = **Apply** that idea with a more concrete plan that solves their particular problem and alleviates the *Darkness*.

D = **Deliver** a happy ending vision for how they will prosper in the *Light* with you if they agree.

Let's take a look at how READ can help you dialogue with purpose in real life by attaching the threads of your personal story to something that you want to make happen:

Scenario #1: Messaging Your Personal Story

This peek behind the curtain of my own backstory incident shows how this Prompt helped me to build the foundation of my narrative. Here's how I lived through the four cycles of the Narrative Arc and faced emotional change and conflict:

- The *Shift* happened when my company was sold, and I needed a new job.
- The *Instability* brought plenty of missteps as I tested new things, including starting my own consulting business and trying to write a book at the same time.
- The *Darkness* came when I was almost finished with the book and realized that the real story was different from the one I was writing, and I had to start over.
- The *Light* came when I finished the book and was filled with new insight into how to combine my business and creative sides.

I went into that incident one way and came out stronger on the other side. Living through the cycles showed me that I have the agility to pivot, the tenacity to see something through, the power to reinvent and to inspire people, and many other descriptive words that led to my Defining Line. So when I'm in a business setting with someone I might want to work with and they ask: "Tell me about yourself," I'm ready. I've done all the prep work on my story and created my READ script in advance so I can then pull out the right story threads in the moment of any conversation to weave my story in the most compelling way. Here's one example that I could use if I'm at the beginning stages of trying to win a new client:

Relate. We are in a moment where everyone needs to reinvent—and when my magazine publishing world imploded, I had to start over like so many others. Yet, I was uncertain about what to do and which way to turn, which mirrors how so many feel about choosing their next, best strategic step.

Ease. What allowed me to move forward was looking inward. My number one career theme was clear—I was always inventing or reinventing something—so this notion hit to finally become the chief innovation officer of *me* rather than for someone else. I realized that I didn't have to choose between two companies to join, I could take an alternate route and build a new career on my own terms. And starting my own business would help to fulfill what that inward glance also revealed—there was a book I needed to write.

Apply. I was fortunate to help many different clients with their business reinventions as I typed my own in the early morning hours. I really did not know where I was going when I began writing but I did know that persevering despite the odds would somehow be meaningful. And that turned out to be true—not only did immersing myself in the world of storytelling reveal untapped personal strengths and unrecognized talents, but it also helped me to discover lessons that could enhance the work world for everyone.

Deliver. Now that *Saturday's Child* became an award-winning book that transformed my life, I realize that this was the story that only I could tell, and it led me to create a new platform to transform others that only I could teach. Now my business and creative expertise inspires professionals to reach their career potential and our collaboration will align you with my powerful process that changes lives and invents successful futures. And that is something every company needs now.

Scenario #2: Pitch

Now let's look at how I used some of my story's building blocks to pitch a different angle for the *Thrive Global* feature on leadership advice:

R = Relate to some shared Shift

Thank you for asking me to participate in *Thrive Global*'s business leadership series but we both need to be sure that what I contribute adds real value to you and your audience. With the glut of digital content, it seems that anything anyone might want to know is already out there—my simple Google search for leadership advice turned up over two million results!

E = Ease the Instability with an idea

You've got me thinking, though, about what I could possibly say that would be different. What if I could come up with a way to connect leadership success to what I learned from my creative journey to write a book?

A = Apply that idea to solve their Darkness

The five lessons I've discovered about storytelling can teach people a replicable process that not only will make them more successful in any field but, by default, better leaders as well. It would be a completely fresh take with much more inherent value than commonplace motivational words.

D = Deliver a vision for the Light afterward

I believe structuring the leadership advice that you're asking for around the storytelling lessons I've learned not only makes them actionable for your audience but benefits *Thrive Global* exponentially. Since you will be the source introducing this new approach, together we will build your audience impressions, content shares, and consumer loyalty.

Scenario #3: Exploratory Conversation

Now let's activate READ for a hypothetical job-hunting scenario where the story threads you are pulling are your talents within the work world. Imagine that you are currently in digital content marketing for a beauty brand, but you want to switch to the wellness industry. You've identified a company you'd like to work for, and connected on LinkedIn with its VP, who has agreed to have an exploratory conversation since you have multiple people in common. You're confident going in because you've done your READ homework and can now tailor the right points for this meeting, including uniting your mission with theirs. Here's how your chat might go:

R = Relate to some shared Shift

Digital Marketing has never been easier, yet with the deluge of commoditized content, I think we could both talk all day about how we're actually facing more hurdles than we ever did before.

E = **Ease** the Instability with an idea

Because the beauty industry is so competitive and fickle, it is always at the forefront of new ideas and cutting-edge techniques. It has been the best possible training ground for me, implanting solutions that will benefit other categories, especially the growing but challenged wellness industry. Now that I'm committed to improving people's lives through better health, your brand intrigues me because of how you embody that same commitment.

A = **Apply** that idea to solve their Darkness

There are beauty levers that I can easily pull for wellness, from mass customization to blending content and commerce most effectively. One of the secrets to connect with audiences and stand-apart from all the noise is to create value-based conversations instead of purely transactional ones—and I know just how to transfer that knowledge to you.

D = **Deliver** a vision for the Light afterward

In my present role, I've doubled responsiveness and revenue in the last three years, and I know that I can do the same for your brand. If you chose to bring my skills and outside-the-category thinking into your organization now or when the time is right, together we will lift sales and help the world to be a healthier place. With your objectives in mind, how could my skills be a fit one day?

Grammar Rules!

READ is a verb and as such, it is active. As you use READ to clarify your message and get you to where you want to go, remember to add a suffix to be sure you end with a call-to-action.

Adding an "S" at the end to form READS will trigger you to "Slide" into asking for what you want. Or an "ING" suffix to form READING will remind you to keep "**I N**eed **G**reat" results in mind.

> So after you Deliver your happy ending, suggest that your listener(s) take the action that will benefit you!

STEP #3: *Animating Your Company's Story*

Unless you are an entrepreneur with your own venture or in corporate communications, you are not responsible for creating your company's story. You are, however, responsible for bringing it to life for others. Whether you are in sales or marketing, IT or HR, manufacturing or distribution, business or product development, part of your role is to convey a company story.

The key to getting comfortable with business storytelling is to fully accept that everyone is always messaging something to incite some sort of action—in other words, you are always "selling," even if you're not in sales. And *how* you do this is crucial to your success.

Ask, Ask, and Ask Again

A sure way to get to great storytelling is by "story-asking." Creative questioning is one of your most powerful secret weapons to shape your messages and tell your most effective stories at work. Intelligence-gathering not only enables you to understand the backstory of anything more completely but also bestows the ideas and solutions that wait within the enlightening answers.

Because this conversational give-and-take is so crucial to your ultimate success, the lessons have reinforced the value of asking the right question to the right person at the right time. And the lessons demonstrate how to frame the open-ended questions that will elicit the most meaningful answers. Still, I find that actively probing for more in meetings and conversations remains a stumbling block for many.

So, I've developed this easy-to-remember acronym—THE WAY—that distills everything I've learned about dialogue as an author, trained journalist, business expert, and coach into a complete, easy-to-remember list of the best open-ended questions and statements. Now you can have a "writer in your pocket" when you're in a discussion with anyone:

T = Tell me ... (about ... more about ... your perspective on, etc.).

H = How do you ... (define the problem ... see this working ... view the best next step, etc.)?

E = Educate me on ... (one thing that needs to change ... one thing you wish could happen, etc.)

W = What ... (do you need ... does success look like ... are your concerns am I missing, etc.)?

A = And what else ... (could make this work .... would improve the result, etc.)?

Y = Yes, and ... (continue acknowledging and then building on the feedback you're receiving).

Insert Yourself

Communicating an idea and its significance in a way that other people can grasp is what writers spend their lives doing. To apply your storytelling skills most effectively, however—and build relationships at the same time—you want to thread your own story to the larger stories of your company and its clients, partners, and customers.

Adding a personal story to your business storytelling that underscores your essence, ethos, or experience will heighten your emotional connection and relatability. The goal here is to be vulnerable while *being discreet* and fully in control of what you actually reveal. This is not at all about oversharing on a personal level—that could be counterproductive in a business situation. Rather, it is about sharing a story that relates to what you're talking about and humanizes you, perhaps by showing how you faced and overcame some adversity. You want to share enough to achieve a united bond through a heartfelt moment or a laugh without losing sight of the point that you are trying to reinforce—you should always keep your quest and the result that you want to achieve front-and-center in your mind.

For example, in Scenario #3's hypothetical above, did the woman recently transform her life in some way that turned her from a beauty enthusiast into a wellness ambassador? Did she have an epiphany after taking up yoga or meditation? Did weight loss or a new fitness routine help reshape her career vision? Bringing the right personal sound-bytes into a business conversation helps the other person understand who you are and recognize the value that you bring.

One way to find that personal connection is to review your answers to the Imagine Prompts and try to uncover the commonalities between your story and your company's. And do the same for any company you want to talk to—for example, if you are pitching a prospective client, find a way to join your or your company's story *to their story*. Express whatever marketplace Shift affects you both so you immediately Relate to the other person and then explain how your company's vision is aligned with theirs. Whenever you are in a messaging mode, your goal is straightforward: make the other person see how you can help them achieve the outcome they want.

Aim High

Another way to optimize your business storytelling is to have exacting standards for how you message your recommendations and results. With your storytelling hat firmly in place, you want to find a way to take the verbal and visual expression of your work to a higher level every single time.

Think about your next PowerPoint or project wrap-up or budget review. Your presentation will be conveying something that you want others to understand, buy into, and appreciate. Writers know that every good story must have an inciting incident in the first ten pages (some would even say on page one) to grab people's attention. So will you drone on with slide after slide of set-up data and analysis? Or will you now immediately get their attention—think the beginning of Chapter One—through an inciting storyline that makes them instantly grasp the risk and possibility of failure if they don't act?

One of the greatest presentation openings ever was produced by the enterprise solutions company, Zuora. They turned all the data into an urgent story that neatly fits into a READ template, one that relates to a Shift and gets buy-in to an idea:

- We are Moving to a Subscription Economy—it is a different relationship-centric era.
- There Will Be Winners and Losers—52% of Fortune 500 companies have disappeared.
- The Winners have a Common Thread—they all provide a subscription experience.
- Zuora is Your Answer—listen to what our customers have to say about their turnarounds.

This *hair-on-fire* opening makes any business audience gasp OMG as they sit up straight and grasp what the stakes are. Once, when I was in corporate marketing, I had to ask for money to fund an initiative I believed was crucial for where we needed to go as a company. My odds for success were slim—it was a million-dollar ask and there were many competing priorities—so I knew I needed to be creative to win the CEO's attention. Then, when I was out shopping for Halloween costumes with my children, I was struck by an idea for how I could open my presentation, offer a glimpse into my personal story for relatability, and demonstrate my own whimsy, creativity, and boldness.

The next day, I went into the high-level executive meeting and began to silently lay out all sorts of plastic weaponry on the gleaming conference table. A sword, battle-ax, knife, shield, and more, all plucked from the costume racks. Everyone was staring at me, confused, until I finally said, "This project is so critical for our future, we are not leaving the room until we agree to fund it." An idle threat, but then I started to weave a story by connecting each weapon to a part of the project in a convincing way—for example, the plastic knife showed how we would be able to slice and dice content for readers and viewers. Long story short, I got people's attention. And I got the money.

No messaging is too small or insignificant to matter, so whenever you're involved in something, be consistently known for great, meaningful output.

Story Intelligence

Whoever tells the best story wins. For your best results, continue building your story intelligence—what I like to call your *SI Quotient*—with these four writing-world tips that will transform your presentations into *SI* winners:

Create a package. Just like a book cover, whatever materials you produce need to have a distinct look, feel, and design that enhances your story. Combine a few keywords with striking visuals to convey your central theme, the tension of the problem, and the solution. Think about how a plot advances and let the ending that you want to achieve be the throughline that guides your presentation's beginning and middle. Open with a high-level expression of the current scenario or problem and follow with the plot points that can move you toward a solution. Always close with benefits and an "ask"—a call-to-action that will get you to the finish line or to next steps.

Build-in emotion. Use your backstory to show how you came to believe what you do so you can transfer those values to your audience. Say "You, we, and us" wherever possible. And remember to include real-world stories like testimonials or team member bios to give credence to what you are communicating, as well as powerful quotes to underscore your points. For example, the unsettling Netflix documentary about technology, *The Social Dilemma*, uses thought-provoking quotes to reinforce its themes, including the opening Sophocles line, "Nothing vast enters the life of mortals without a curse." Provocative lines continue throughout, such as, "There are only two industries that call their customers users: illegal drugs and software" that heighten any viewer's understanding.

Know the storylines. As best you can, be sure to know the story of whoever you're talking to (and their brand if it's external). Grab hold of their big picture narrative and positioning from the "About Us" tab on their website; read their press releases; dig for their distinct brand identity, ethos, and character; and search for their business development and marketing initiatives—from content to sponsorships to brand partners—to gain more context. Information, as they say, is always power.

Keep up the pacing. Every conversation has a rhythm and is a dance of sorts. To make any discussion successful, try to harmonize with the other person by being alert and aware of cues. Pause to listen after any statement you make and then pay close attention to the other person's response. As we learned with follow-ups, you can then insert their answer, along with any insight it sparked, into what you say next. Make your questions open-ended throughout and be in active listening mode—whatever they say, the other person is always going to inform and advance your own path forward.

Activating READ for Your Brand or Product

To begin, keep these top two business storytelling rules front-and-center:

- **Personal.** You are the H of your life but at work, you are a supporting character. The story isn't about you, it's all about the company you work for—or your client or partner— and their goals and needs. Just keep them on your page one and everyone's story will improve.
- **Company.** Winning businesses understand that they are not the H of their work story either. They too have a supporting character role in service to another. Remember our company EDIT? For any business, the *customer* is the H who sits at the center of their story. As the supporting character, the company acts as a wise mentor who guides the H to a better place through whatever that company produces. Any business that loses sight of this fundamental story will lose their way.

With all this in mind, these final four business scenes activate the READ formula to demonstrate its effectiveness with concepts, brand expansions, and launches. Let each scenario spark how you can use READ at work when you want to formulate a new idea, bring a new product to market, or broaden your business.

Scenario #1: Concept

Remember the flurry of post-pandemic TV commercials that appeared in 2020 as companies tried to stay relevant and still sell their products? The big story question they had to answer was: How can we help people stay sane and continue to choose us while there are massive constraints on our society? Let's pretend we're under the gun to present a solution to the media director of an automotive company during that time. An effective ZOOM call to get buy-in using a READ lens might have gone something like this:

Relate. We're all feeling the uncertainty of this pandemic, and the isolation it causes is putting the emotional and physical wellbeing of every household at risk. Fair warning, one of my three children might suddenly barge in asking me to help solve a math problem or find the Doritos, so fingers crossed that we sail through.

Ease. Now, about wellbeing. We asked ourselves: What if our vehicles actually became even more important to our customers as the embodiment of personal freedom in these unprecedented times?

Apply. This storyboard for a 60-second spot shows a harried couple with young and restless children going about their crazy day inside their house, working from home and helping their kids with remote schooling—until they finally all slip into their car, lock the doors, and take off for a safe open-air adventure to leave the world's troubles behind.

Deliver. Their faces beam with happiness and their stress melts away as they frolic and reconnect with one another. Because their car has taken them away to beauty and nature, each one of them is better equipped to face the uncertainty of tomorrow. At the very least, our message will convey that we understand and care about our customers. At the very best, people will consider a new car purchase now to give them an escape and flexibility, which will drive sales.

Scenario #2: Product Launch

Another example to show you READ-in-action is the now-familiar men's fashion brand _UNTUCKit_ that came out of nowhere and grew to a $200 million company seemingly overnight. Let's put founder Chris Riccobono's launch conversation into a READ template:

Relate. Although I never wanted to wear a tie, I also hated casual dressing because my shirt was always wrong and long. You probably know what I mean because when I asked every single man I knew, they all felt exactly the same way.

Ease. Since casual dressing is here to stay, I wondered if we could solve this problem that every man has by inventing an entirely new shirt—one that was simply the perfect length to leave untucked.

Apply. The moment we prototyped and tested this shorter design, we knew we were about to revolutionize the entire shirt industry. Feedback was so positive that we decided to take on all the risk and launch an e-commerce direct-to-consumer brand. With a small friends and family investment, we built a profitable, scalable brand out of the gate that has blown past every single projection and turned a legacy industry on its head.

Deliver. Men come in all shapes and sizes, but that's not how traditional shirts are made. We've totally re-engineered the casual dress shirt to have the perfect untucked length and that just-right fit so they can help every guy look his best—always.

Scenario #3: Product Launch

SPANX Founder Sara Blakely has widely shared the inspiring origin story of her billion-dollar brand. It's a classic that neatly fits into the READ template to further show how we can shape and animate a business story:

Relate. My career was full of fits and starts and not at all what I envisioned for myself. You and probably everyone else we know has had similar feelings. After a particularly rock-bottom day, it was time to reassess and ask myself some serious questions.

Ease. I realized that the only strength I had was sales. As I wondered what I could do next with that one skill, I wrote down: "I want to invent a product that I can sell to millions of people that will make them feel better." That's what I envisioned even though I didn't know what the product was.

Apply. Two years later, I cut the feet out of control-top pantyhose to look my best while wearing white pants to a party. And suddenly, there was the product. I drove around to manufacturers and was escorted out through many doors until one said, "Sara, I have decided to help you make your crazy idea."

Deliver. Then, I had to find a way to sell them. I finally got my first big account, Neiman Marcus, by saying, "I've invented a product that will change the way your customers wear clothes and I need ten minutes of your time." And that was the start of a phenomenon that does help millions of people feel better every day—including you.

Scenario #4: Expansion

And finally, here's a script for some business-building of my own as I look to expand *Authorize It!* workshops beyond corporations to colleges. These advance talking points help me to frame my conversations with different career counselors:

Relate. As my workshops inspire employees to greater heights, I'm constantly reminded just how much their mindsets, expectations, and needs at work are dramatically changing. One of the biggest hand-wringing problems my corporate clients have is the actual readiness of their entry-level employees. Since you're preparing the next generation workforce, you must be thinking about these issues as well, just like the companies your students will graduate to.

Ease. After seeing the problems with onboarding and motivating entry-level employees over and over, I suddenly realized that companies were stuck trying to fix these issues *after* the fact. To truly tackle the problem, we needed to get to the students *before* they entered the business world.

Apply. I've adapted my *Authorize It!* corporate workshop for colleges to give graduating seniors the real-world perspective and skills that they need to succeed. I piloted workshops at three colleges and the positive feedback from the participants and the institutions has been beyond what I had envisioned.

Deliver. Especially with today's marketplace uncertainty, it has never been more important for colleges to demonstrate their value in terms of the student's prospects and lives post-college. Together we can ensure that your graduates are fully prepared to succeed as they begin their careers. How can I help you help them by fitting a workshop into your curriculum?

Whether you are crafting or telling your own story or your company's, READ is the framework that will polish your storytelling and enable you to win people over, encourage them to contribute and collaborate, and amplify your success all along the way. If you have a quota to hit, a client to convince, or a team member who needs to climb on board, *think like a writer and authorize your situation.* You have the power to shape your narrative and achieve your quest—and be the H who adapts and thrives wherever life leads.

Authorize It! is a lifelong process, and the sooner you begin, the sooner you will see the impact. I hope that all you have learned motivates you to become an independent, self-directed H who can live up to your true potential even in these erratic times. The innate value of the five lessons—and how to pull it all together for the stories you're telling—will only increase over time as you continue to grow, recalibrate your quest, and ascend from wherever you are to do whatever you choose.

There is no denying that awareness of this new approach—and of yourself—launches the incredibly hard work of changing thoughts, patterns, and habits that no longer suit, and then inserting new and better behaviors in their place. Because any transformation is challenging, a whole industry of experts has been born to help with personal evolution as well as business evolution. So, if you'd like more in-depth support, as a starting point check the Resources at the end of this book for further reading, listening, and viewing.

If this book resonated with you, please consider leaving a review on Amazon and, of course, you can also send me a direct message on LinkedIn, through my website: deborahburnsauthor.com, or on social: deborah_l_burns on Instagram or @deborahburnsauthor on Facebook. I'd also love to hear how thinking like a writer has impacted your career—knowing how it has made a positive difference in your life will turn this into a happy ending for me as well.

With all my best wishes for the ultimate success of your journey,
Deborah

P.S. Read-on for the last installment of *Authorize It! Live* and how Sharon turned her career—and her life—around.

Authorize It! Live

One Year Later—Sharon's Story

Now that we have tied all the lessons together to *authorize* the stories you're telling, let's close out *Authorize It! Live* with a final Sharon check-in. With each lesson, we added additional layers of insight to fully answer her frequently asked question but now, at her twelve-month mark, it was *my turn* to finally ask Sharon a question: How did thinking like a writer impact your career?

Sharon's Testimonial

"I look back at the person I was then, and my jaw drops. *Who was that girl?* I can't say that my career has changed all that much—yet. I'm still at the same company, and in the same job. But I can say that *I have changed*, and that's the absolute best aspect. And because of the dramatic changes within myself, what I do for a living is on the way to changing.

I got started with *Authorize It!* because I had heard someone describe it as a "little jewel," and for me, it's been just that. Thinking like a writer was easy to grasp, unlike all the mindfulness speak that loses me, or the positive-thinking affirmations that feel a little silly. This made sense, I could feel it, and I immediately realized how true it is.

The most important aspect of the program was how each one of these lessons opened me up to a new approach in their own way. With *Embrace the Narrative Arc*, learning about the cycles changed my perspective and I still think about the four ingredients of a story every single day. Realizing that I held the power through my actions, reactions, and expectations was a wake-up call. When I adopted the qualities of an H mentality, I didn't announce anything at the office, I just did things differently. Soon, I was getting more compliments for my enthusiasm or for coming up with a suggestion to solve something, and that recognition has been so encouraging.

With *Understand Your Characters*, I leaped right into the deep end of the pool. I loved fictionalizing myself with the Protagonist Profile and looking very honestly at what might have made me so resistant to things (yes, I am, and I can say that out loud now), and what I've struggled with (not going to share those things here, but I now have much more clarity). And I loved building on each lesson's *What's My Story?* Prompt to go deeper and get into storytelling mode about myself.

With *Welcome Conflict*, I had never looked at its positive side, but what really blew my mind in Lesson Three were the insights about the inner antagonist. I also had never thought much about how I might have been in my own way, and because of this section, I've given up comparisons (for the most part!) and can better handle the thoughts and emotions that make me feel defeated. It's easier now to get around obstacles or at least see the bumps in the road as important to my development.

Seek the Unconventional was a lesson I also really needed because I tend to be traditional in how I approach things. When I read it, it just made so much sense that it switched something on for me. Because I was so inspired, I now ask myself about everything: Is this different? Is this unusual? If it's not, I move on.

Step Into the Unknown. You were right in your assessment—I was waiting for something to come to me and I wasn't taking the initiative I could have. Now, I'm no longer waiting for something to just appear, I'm churning stuff around every day. I took that first step by signing up for a non-credited finance class just to see since I've always been good at math. I haven't found my passion just yet but being in the thick of new things has planted a seed.

Authorize It!: Tell Your Stories. This was the IT moment for me! I re-read how it all comes together with messaging and expressing at least five times and I'm sure it will remain a handy resource. To me, activating it all with the READ tool changed the way I think. My work has one hundred percent improved because I'm so much more thoughtful about all my output, and being able to summarize myself was transforming for me. I now think that one day I'd like to be a financial advisor and I even came up with a Defining Line—*To help every woman's future by planting the right financial seeds now.* This has set me on a new quest and life feels much more promising.

Meantime, because my positive changes have been noticed by others—and because I communicate with READ in mind—I'm blooming where I'm planted.

I even got tapped by management for an innovation team! When I was chosen as the leader of a multi-disciplinary task force charged with tackling a specific business challenge, I was overjoyed by the recognition but also extremely nervous.

To ease that feeling, I decided to structure our eight-week mission around all I had learned from *Authorize It!*:

For the first five weeks, each session addressed an aspect of the problem through one lesson's teaching—we asked the right questions to get to new answers and, by the end, we could definitely feel the power of activating the five lessons together.

In week six, we worked on telling a new company story with READ. In the seventh session we came up with recommendations, and in the eighth session, we put together an exciting presentation for management.

The result? Our executive team committed to moving forward with all our recommendations, and there has been a new normal for me. The team's work was shared company-wide, boosting my visibility and morale—plus I got a small bonus! I was also given the opportunity to be a part of bringing one of the recommendations to life to further expand my horizons. Between leading the team and then adding a new project, I'm working harder than ever, but seeing how far I've progressed makes it all worthwhile. I'm on my way … and that's the greatest feeling of all.

Resources—Recommended Reading, Watching, and Listening

Big Magic, Elizabeth Gilbert

Claim Your Power, Mastin Kipp

Daring Greatly, Brené Brown

David and Goliath, Malcolm Gladwell

Everything is Figureoutable, Marie Forleo

How Great Leaders Inspire Action, TED Talk, Simon Sinek

How the World Sees You, Sally Hogshead

How to Fail: Everything I've Ever Learned From Things Going Wrong, Elizabeth Day

How to Fail, Podcast, Elizabeth Day

Influence: The Psychology of Persuasion, Robert B. Cialdini, PhD

Magic Lessons, Podcast, Elizabeth Gilbert

Make a Name for Yourself, Robin Fisher Roffer

MasterClass, Margaret Atwood, masterclass.com

Maybe You Should Talk to Someone, Lori Gottlieb

Reframe: Shift the Way You Work, Innovate, and Think, Mona Patel

Re:Invent Your Life! What are You Waiting For?, Kathi Sharpe-Ross

Self Made, Nely Galán

Squircle: A New Way to Think for a New World, Francis Cholle

Still Writing, Dani Shapiro

Stop Searching for Your Passion, TEDxKC Video, Terri Trespicio

Strategize to Win, Carla A. Harris

The Artist's Way, Julia Cameron

The Beautiful No, Shari Salata

The Big Life, Ann Shoket

The Charged Life With Brendon Burchard, Podcast

The Creative Fire, Clarissa Pinkola Estes

The Creativity Leap: Unleash Curiosity, Improvisation, and Intuition at Work, Natalie Nixon

The Dance of Anger, Harriet Lerner, PhD

The Four Agreements, Don Miguel Ruiz, Peter Coyote

The Four Tendencies, Gretchen Rubin

The Hero with a Thousand Faces, Joseph Campbell

The Hero's 2 Journeys, Audible Originals with Michael Hauge and
   Christopher Vogler

*The Myth of the Nice Girl: Achieving a Career You Want Without Becoming a
   Person You Hate*, Fran Hauser

*The New Rules of Work: The Muse Playbook for Navigating The Modern
   Workplace*, Alexandra Cavoulacos and Kathryn Minshew

The Path Made Clear: Your Life's Direction and Purpose, Oprah Winfrey

The Power of Meaning, Emily Esfahani Smith

The Seven Spiritual Laws of Success, Deepak Chopra

The War of Art, Steven Pressman

The Work, Byron Katie

Think Like an Artist, Will Gompert

This is Your Life With Michael Hyatt, Podcast

What I Know for Sure, Oprah Winfrey

Why People Don't Heal and How They Can, Caroline Myss

Getting the Love You Want, Harville Hendrix Ph.D. and Helen LaKelly
   Hunt PhD

Year of Yes: How to Dance It Out, Stand In the Sun and Be Your Own Person,
   Shonda Rhimes

VIA Institute on Character, Character Strengths Survey, viacharacter.org

Acknowledgments

"Some people are in your life for a reason, a season, or a lifetime." Often heard because they are the truest of words. I remain grateful for all of the people in my life, no matter their category, and no matter how hard some of their lessons might have been for me to learn. All of them—*all of them*—got me to where I am now, here with you.

When each of us looks at our Narrative and Character Arcs we see that our stories have taken us on unexpected journeys as they continue to unfold. Like yours, mine is shaped by all those who came before and all those who cross our paths now.

With appreciation for my beloved parents and aunts, and for their continued inspiration even though they are gone: Dorothy, Jasper, Lena, and Lilly. You made me who I am.

With heartfelt thanks and love for my cherished family: Robert, Richard, Elizabeth, Edward, Theresa, Corrado, Emilia, Baby-girl-to-be (and whoever else might be on the way). You give my life meaning.

With gratitude for the family, friends, and wise ones around me who I've been fortunate enough to have in my life. Like stars, there are too many of you to thank individually. So, I can only hope that I've managed to convey just how important you are to me. Know that you remain a part of my night sky, and with every glance upward, I am reminded of my constellation of sparkling dots connecting in serendipitous ways. You all have breathed life into this idea and through it, you've given my life a new purpose.

Acclaim for Author Deborah Burns

Saturday's Child **Awards**: IPPY Gold, Reader Views Silver, Best Book Finalist, Shelf Unbound Notable

Saturday's Child **Features**: *The Hollywood Reporter, Forbes, Entertainment Weekly, Parade, PopSugar, Refinery29, Brit + Co, Thrive Global, Medium, Yahoo, Scary Mommy, Next Tribe, SheKnows, Books on the Subway, Ms. Career Girl, NY Post,* and *LA Times.*

Saturday's Child **Praise**:

"A fascinating mother-daughter tale loaded with the realities of perfection, perception, identity, and the choices we make. An intergenerational story for the ages."
—Rochelle Weinstein, national best-selling author of
Somebody's Daughter

"In her searingly honest memoir, Deborah Burns unpacks what it means to be the daughter of a mistaken-for-a-movie-star mother who refuses to be defeated by life, no matter its disappointments. At once painful and uplifting, and rich with period detail, you will fall in love with both generations."
—Sally Koslow, international best-selling author of
Another Side of Paradise

"With a journalist's eye and a poet's hand, the author conveys the unique texture of her glamorous mother's elusive love. Heartbreaking and hopeful, searing and soulful, *Saturday's Child* is unputdownable—this generation's *Terms of Endearment.*"
—Meghann Foye, author of *Meternity*

"A cinematic memoir that reads like fiction, with lush, elegant prose that belies a raw, honest narrative of a daughter coming to terms with the narcissistic mother whom she idealized. An unforgettable journey of discovery, understanding, and self-love."

—Lisa Anselmo, author of *My (Part-Time) Paris Life: How Running Away Brought Me Home*

"A universal tale of family and the quest for belonging; of reconciling the secrets we keep with the desire for truth; and of discovering that the unconditional love we all crave from others can ultimately be found inside ourselves."

—Holly C. Corbett, author of *The Lost Girls: Three Friends, Four Continents, One Unconventional Detour Around the World.*

"Mesmerizing. A must-read for any daughter who's ever tried to figure out where her mother ends and she begins."

—Lynnda Pollio, author of *Trusting the Currents*

"A beautifully written love letter to a fascinating mother. I was immediately drawn in by both the prose and the mysteries at the heart of this unique mother-daughter relationship."

—Andrea Jarrell, author of *National Book Critics Circle* Award-nominee *I'm the One Who Got Away*

"Riveting and affecting; timeless and timely—a stunning debut."

—Bethany Ball, author of *What to Do About the Solomons*

"A poignant, candid exploration of the bond between mother and daughter. In allowing herself to see her mother as a real person, flaws and all, Burns not only sets herself free—she shows the rest of us how to do the same."

—Gayle Brandeis, author of *The Art of Misdiagnosis: Surviving My Mother's Suicide*

"Deborah Burns fearlessly reveals the hidden truths of a compelling and challenging mother-daughter relationship. Vividly written and thoroughly rewarding!"
  —Barbara Novack, Writer-in-Residence, Molloy College, author of Pulitzer Prize-nominated novel *J. W. Valentine*

"In this captivating memoir, the relationship between an unconventional and fiercely independent mother and the daughter who idolized her is revealed in all its complexity. A story of identity, self-discovery, and forgiveness."
  —Jennifer Kitses, author of the novel *Small Hours*

"A heartfelt tale of love, honor, and becoming ... wise and wonderful."
  —Agapi Stassinopolous, author of *Wake Up to the Joy of You*

170

About the Author

Deborah's story has always been about invention and reinvention —she's lived those two keywords throughout her career as a women's media Chief Innovation Officer, a leader of brands like *ELLE Décor* and *Metropolitan Home,* and an industry consultant. And she's also lived them in a life full of creative twists and turns that led to writing the award-winning memoir, *Saturday's Child.*

The experience of becoming an author transformed her life once more and illuminated the path to this second book. Now, Deborah helps businesses and people invent and reinvent their companies, careers, and lives. *Her Authorize It!* corporate and college workshops and online course nurture talent, inspire personal and professional development, and help everyone live up to their potential with more successful careers.

The author lives on Long Island, New York, with her husband Robert—and with their three children and two precious granddaughters nearby.

Made in the USA
Middletown, DE
13 April 2021